FROM
Death to
Disparity

FROM *Death to Disparity*

ELIZABETH R. BARBIERE

Bethanne Publishers
Baltimore, Maryland

From Death to Disparity
Elizabeth Barbiere

ISBN 0-9774106-0-9

Published by Bethanne Publishers
118 E. Clement Street
Baltimore, MD 21230

Dedication

To the loving memory of my brother, Ralph Wayne Barbiere, without whose life story, this book would have never been possible.

Prologue

It was July. It was nearly four in the morning. All was still in Tunis. There was no sign of life or movement, except perhaps for a few undernourished cats stalking the overloaded the trash pails in the Medina, finding what tidbits they could to stay alive. The night lights shined into the fully blossomed trees along the main Avenue, with no breeze or wind disturbing them. The moon was almost full. It was comfortably warm. All was still. There was no one in sight. No one.

There was no one, that is, until a girl came into view. Anna was running. She seemed to be coming from one end of town and headed toward the opposite side of the city. When she reached the main avenue, however, she stopped. The night lights shining into her face showed a terrified expression. She was stark white. She looked around as if she did not know her whereabouts (although she had been there a thousand times before). Her fear was not fear of being alone, though, but a sort of hysteria. She was, indeed, in shock.

After a few moments of rest, she continued on to the Medina. Now, instead of searching endlessly, she seemed familiar with her surroundings. as if she knew exactly where she was going. Without hesitation, she took a shortcut into a small alley. It was dark and damp inside, and the ground pavement was uneven. But she did not slow her pace. She crossed it as quickly as possible, groping her way through the dark and narrow space. When she came out of the alley, she arrived at a secondary road close to where she was going. Now it was still quite dark outside for there were no public night lights in the Medina.

Anna turned the corner and found the exact door she wanted. She entered a dark outside hallway which led to a courtyard or an open pavement where laundry and dry goods would be put out during the daytime. Again she stopped for a few seconds, her eyes darting around nervously. Within less than a minute, she scurried out of the courtyard and climbed a nearby staircase to the second floor to a group of separate rooms. It was even darker in this closed area. Nearly stumbling several times, she crossed the upper floor and hurried to the door she was looking for. Without self-consciousness, she banged on it.

"Noureddine!" Getting no answer, she knocked again. "Noureddine, let me in," she begged in French.

Finally, her calls were heard. Noureddine, alone in the room, flicked on a small lamp on the floor beside his bed. His room consisted of four dirty walls, a bed, and a table and chair, beside which were a bunch of books and papers piled carelessly on the floor. Noureddine, groggy and naked to the waist, reached for a pair of blue jeans on the chair beside him. He slid them on under his sheets and stumbled out of bed. Without even looking at the clock next to his lamp, he hustled to the door, which was closed in three different places. He unlatched the security locks and opened it. Standing at the door was Anna, looking as pale as a ghost.

"What's going on? What time is it?" he asked in French.

Anna was breathing hard. "He's dead," she gasped. "My brother is dead."

"What?" Noureddine was shocked, but baffled.

"My parents called about an hour ago. I guess they didn't know what time it was over here. They told me he's dead. It's all over, Noureddine."

Noureddine was beginning to understand, but for Anna's sake he kept a facade of confusion. "Look," he said, "I don't understand, but come in." His voice sounded calm and reassuring. "Come in and tell me what happened."

Anna did not like Noureddine's depressing surroundings and certainly had no need for them now. "No, I don't feel like being inside," she said, which was also true. "Let's just go out to a cafe or bar or something. It doesn't matter where, but let's just go out."

Later, Anna and Noureddine found themselves in a typical Arabic cafe-bar; the only kind that was open at that time of the morning. It was now about 5 a.m. Day was breaking, and the city was becoming animated, with many people already going to work. Anna had calmed down and was thinking much more rationally than before. She was finishing her third beer. She sat back in the wooden chair, facing Noureddine.

"This is the end," she said.

"The end of what?"

"Of everything," she answered.

Chapter 1

The year was 1978. The month was September. Anna, her brother Paul, and their parents were in New York on one of their visits to see relatives in Brooklyn. Everyone on the paternal side of Anna's family was brilliant, industrious, ambitious, and extremely driven. Their determination to succeed knew no bounds, and they were confident in their accomplishments.

Anna did not feel terribly competitive as far as her extended family was concerned. She had long ago concluded that they could live their lives, and she would live hers. Paul, on the other hand, was quite affected by the family mentality. Uncomfortable in his relatives' presence, he felt inferior and inadequate next to his paternal cousins, as if they were accomplishing more in their lives than he was in his. He also felt extremely envious of their fantastic drive and intelligence.

During the visit, a forced conversation between Paul and his cousin Andy, a law-school student, revealed Paul's feelings.

"So this is your last year at Harvard?" Paul asked self-consciously.

"Yeah, I'm finally getting out," Andy replied, trying to sound casual.

"What are you going to do afterward?" Paul continued, as if he really wanted to know.

"Oh, I'm probably going to go into my uncle's law firm. I guess I can get a good start there."

Andy wasn't bragging—he didn't need to. He had enough going for him as it was. But Paul didn't want to hear this any more than Andy wanted to tell it. It hurt him too much. For the time being, Paul was doing reasonably well. He had been hired by one of the biggest computer companies in the world and had recently bought a fifty-year-old mansion—not bad for a young man of 26. However, this would change in the course of time. Perhaps Paul knew all along that Andy's goals and intentions were more sound than his own.

The whole family had come together that day for Sunday dinner. While in the living room, Paul overheard a conversation between two of his cousins. Darlene, married to a doctor, had her master's degree from Columbia University. She was asking her younger cousin, Tommy, what he was thinking of majoring in once he started college that fall.

"Premed," he said with complete self-assurance.

"Oh, another doctor in the family!" Darlene responded. "How nice."

How nice, Paul silently mimicked his cousin. How utterly divine. All he knew was that he just didn't fit in with their jet-set lifestyle. If he could let it go the way Anna had already done, he would have been much happier for it. But instead, he insisted on letting his cousins' success affect him, in spite of the fact that he knew he didn't have it in himself to rival them.

While Anna's aunt was busy preparing the main meal, Anna helped out by making the salad. She started by tearing a head of lettuce apart and throwing the fragments into a bowl, one by one. Afterward, she chopped up some tomatoes, leaving the juice all over the table, and added them. She did same with two whole onions. Then she tore open a bag of baby carrots and dumped the whole thing into the mixture. To prepare the dressing, she started with some

5

olive oil in a smaller bowl. She took a couple of lemons and cut them up on the table as well. As she squeezed the lemon juice into the olive oil, quite a few seeds fell into the bowl. No problem, Anna thought. She just fished them out with her fingers.

Next, Anna went to the cupboard and got out about five different spices. Opening the small containers one by one, she shook each of the spices into the dressing mixture in exorbitant amounts, and of course, added salt and pepper. Then she took a large spoon and mixed everything together. When all the ingredients looked thoroughly combined, she poured them into the salad bowl. Once everything was combined, it seemed as if there was more seasoning than salad. Oh well, Anna thought. It would be a new experience for everybody. So without hesitation, Anna picked up the bowl, carried it into the dining room, and set it down.

As soon as the rest of the dinner was prepared and put out on the table, everybody went into the dining room, sat down, and began eating. Most of them started with the salad. Soon Anna's uncle, sitting at the head of the table, threw out a random question.

"Who made the salad?" he asked.

"I did," Anna responded.

"Annie (her most popular nickname), it's delicious," he complimented her.

"Thank you," she said, but then she started thinking to herself. Oh dear. It's a good thing he didn't see me make it.

By now attention had switched to Anna. Anna's aunt, a rather prudent woman, was curious about her niece's future plans. "Annie," she asked, sounding almost fearful, "where is this place you're going?"

"Tunisia," Anna answered. "It's in North Africa."

Robert, Anna's father, interrupted. "I don't know why on earth you would want to go there. I mean, I couldn't think of a place more dangerous for a girl to go to alone."

"Dad, we've been through all this before. I just want to get away. I want to see something different. I want to experience something new."

"Yeah, but a Moslem country? You're going to get raped and murdered."

This was not the first time Anna had been told that by her father, and she felt that she needed to hear it again like she needed a hole in the head.

"Dad," she said, clenching her teeth, "if you say that one more time, I'm going to cancel my plans and get a job at a fast food place near you. Is that what you want?"

"You know it isn't, Annie. I just want you to be safe. That's all."

"I'm sure I will be. I can take care of myself, you know." Anna dropped the subject.

Actually, one of the reasons for this trip to New York was to see Anna off at Kennedy Airport. She would be leaving the next day for Tunis. As always, the airport was overcrowded, to the point where just finding parking took about half an hour. But once they found a place to leave the car, Paul, Anna, and their parents got out, retrieved Anna's luggage from the trunk, and went into the terminal.

Once Anna had checked her luggage and confirmed her flight reservation, her parents and brother bade her their last "farewell" and left the airport. Then it was only a matter of time until Anna's flight number would be called. Finally, after about a forty-five minute wait, it was announced that the plane to Tunis was ready to board. Anna grabbed her coat and handbag and proceeded to board the plane from inside the terminal. As soon as she found her seat and had gotten comfortable, Anna sat back and began to relax. Soon, the "No Smoking" and "Fasten Seat Belts" signs were flashed on in the cabins. Then Anna felt the plane begin a rugged take-off. Before she knew it, they were in the air and on their way.

The entire trip took about nine hours. Anna was able to get some sleep during part of it. She wasn't particularly looking forward to what she was going to encounter once she arrived. With all the comments and warnings she'd gotten before she left, her apprehension was certainly understandable. As the plane approached the city of Tunis, it started a gradual descent, and the signs in the cabins flashed on again. An announcement said they would soon be landing. Hearing this, the passengers confined themselves to their seats but waited impatiently for the trip to end. Yet it was at least another twenty minutes before the plane began a final descent. Its wheels hit the ground several times in a rough landing before gliding to a full stop. At last, the passengers were free to get off the airplane. One pushed after another as they lined up in the aisle. Anna just let them file out before even trying to get in line.

After getting off the plane, Anna went to reclaim her baggage, walking over to the conveyor belt where all the luggage was being delivered. Finding her two suitcases on it right away, she picked them off the line and went directly to customs, where her passport was to be checked and her entry date stamped. Here Anna again felt nervous, as she did not like any encounter with men in uniforms. The officer in charge asked her what her profession would be in Tunisia.

"Professor," she answered in French.

The officer looked surprised to see that Anna was so young to have such a high position but let her pass just the same.

Tunisia, though a Moslem country, had been a French colony before its recent independence. There, most of the younger generation spoke French as well as Arabic. Having spent a year in Paris after graduating from college, Anna had a good command of that language and spoke it with very little foreign accent. She knew absolutely no Arabic, and in Tunisia they spoke very little English. So in this country she would be communicating mostly in French.

It was nearly two in the afternoon before Anna finally got outside. Everything she needed to do in the airport had taken time, and Anna had also eaten lunch in one of the coffee shops there. But finally she got out of the place and was now standing at a stop waiting for the bus to come and take her into the city. While still at the airport, things seemed rather familiar to Anna, and there was generally an international atmosphere. But she knew that the worst impact of all was yet to come.

Eventually the bus came and stopped in front of her. Anna climbed up first, hauling her two overloaded suitcases in along with her. Then many people, mostly men, started crowding in one after another around her. The more cramped the bus became, the more uncomfortable Anna felt. She was not sure why. Perhaps it was her imagination. Perhaps she had heard too many stories about the overly suppressed sexuality in countries like these, and now she was overreacting to this apparent impression. Still, as a result of all this closeness, Anna could not help but feel ill at ease.

It was about a half hour's ride to the city of Tunis. The whole time, Anna was wary. But wary of what? she thought. Wary of everything. Anna was wary of the physical proximity she was already experiencing. She was wary of anybody of the male sex approaching her for any reason. She was wary of the considerable language barrier that she would have with the older people there (those who did not speak French). But most of all, Anna was wary of the country itself. What would it be like? she wondered. How would it affect her? This she would soon find out.

Meanwhile, somehow interrupting this disquietude, was the view of certain towns and villages, which she found absolutely fascinating. Most of them consisted of small concrete houses and apartments, with dirt streets and sidewalks separating them. Contrary to what Anna had anticipated, the landscape between these towns seemed to contain a lot of vegetation, almost all of it exceptionally bountiful with grass and tiny green plants. For some reason, Anna had expected that this part of the country would be largely barren, with little housing or development in the cities. Instead, the area contained clusters of what looked more like well-defined districts and communities. The houses within these developments were mostly white concrete buildings designed for a tropical climate. Again, this perplexed Anna, since she had always considered the weather in North Africa to be dry and unyielding.

Another thing that surprised her was the large number of people who lived within the small districts on the outskirts of Tunis. Not many people lived between the cities, except perhaps for a few peasants working their farmland. The relatively small towns, however, seemed full of residents, most of whom were young adults and children. From the few things she saw during her short ride, Anna got the impression that these suburbs consisted of people who were all of the same social class. Little did she know, though, that when she got to Tunis, she would see things from an entirely different perspective.

Once they entered the city limits, Anna figured that this was as good a place as any to get off the bus and start looking for a hotel. The fact that she didn't even have a place to stay didn't help Anna's outlook at all. She certainly did not relish the idea of looking for a room in some dwelling she was not familiar with—a place she didn't know the cost of and that she wasn't even sure was safe. Nonetheless, this was as good a place as any to get out and start looking for a room.

As soon as she got off the bus, she set her suitcases down and just stood there for a few seconds, looking around her. This was the city of Tunis, and this would be her home for at least a year. This is what she would experience day in and day out.

On first impression, Anna did not get the idea that Tunis was much different than any big city in the U.S.—it was clean, modern, and convenient. The streets were densely populated with men and women dressed in modern attire. There seemed to be the usual bustling to be found in any densely inhabited environment. The movement of the vehicles was downright nerve racking, and though there were many cars on the roads, all the buses were jam-packed with people as well. The architecture in the city consisted of mostly well-designed apartment and office buildings, which would inevitably be expensive to rent. It also had the uniquely cosmopolitan atmosphere typical of any big town in any country. It was like any normal, important city. It was also the capital.

Anna soon shook herself out of her initial reverie and began looking for a place to stay. That alone took well over an hour, as having two suitcases, a tote bag, and a purse to carry around made the task all the more difficult. Meanwhile, people stared at Anna as she dragged herself down the city streets and sidewalks, finding it necessary to stop every so often to catch her breath. When she finally did find a hotel, it was undoubtedly an expensive one. The four others she had checked had no vacancies.

After she left her passport with the clerk at the lobby, a bellhop helped Anna with her baggage. The two of them squeezed the luggage into a tiny elevator and rode up to the third floor. The bellhop was a small, decrepit old man who spoke broken French. This alone made it hard for Anna to communicate with him. He was also quite nervous and fidgity. As soon as he had placed everything in Anna's room, he almost hurried to the door, closing it cautiously behind him. Anna stared at the man as he was going out. Knowing the basic customs of older people in countries like these, she had a fairly good hunch about why he was in such a rush to leave.

Needless to say, by this time Anna was exhausted. From the time she had left New York to the moment she was able to settle into the hotel, the trip had taken her nearly fourteen hours, during which time she had slept only a little on the plane. So all she wanted to do now was rest. Anna removed her silk blouse and blue jeans, then stretched out on her bed and turned on a small lamp standing on a nearby night table. To help herself unwind, Anna picked up a magazine relating to French fashion and social issues. Not very interesting, she soon concluded, putting it back where she found it.

One could easily say that Anna was a very appealing young woman. Physically, she was petite and voluptuous. Her thick brown hair draped across her white shoulders. She had blue eyes and an extremely soft, fair complexion, which was already a noticeable contrast to the olive-skinned Arabs, who prevailed as the majority of the population in Tunisia. Socially, Anna could be intimate and personable with anybody really close to her. Detached relationships and cold façades meant nothing to her. Anna was also extremely sensuous, though sexual activity was not indispensable to her. She liked to get to know a man to the fullest degree before she could really call him a friend or a lover. Intellect before sex was her idea of a true relationship. But most of all, Anna was astute and adventurous. As far as her ambitions for the future were concerned, the sky was the limit.

The reason Anna had come to Tunis was because she had a contract to be a teacher there. She was supposed to be a professor of English as a foreign language. A professor, she recalled. Anna was a young woman only twenty-three years of age. It didn't even cross her mind at the time that this was a position which might turn out to be far over her head. Anna didn't want to think about that now. She just wanted to travel, she wanted to work and, most of all, she wanted to expand and develop.

As Anna was relaxing in her hotel room, she thought back to a conversation she'd had with her mother not long before they left for New York. They were sitting in a restaurant where they usually ate on Sunday afternoons. Actually, it was her mother who brought up the subject of Anna's future.

"Do you even know where you're going to stay once you get to Tunis?" Louise asked.

"No," Anna replied. "I have no idea where I'm going to stay."

"But don't you think that's a little risky?" Louise said. "After all, you can't sleep out in the gutter, and you can't ask just anybody to put you up in a country like that."

Anna resented her mother's obvious intent to prove her incapable of making it on her own. "Mother, dear," she said, "I guess I'll have to cross that bridge when I come to it. I'll have a job, which means I'll have some money, which means I'll find a place to stay. It's as simple as that."

"But how long do you think that will last? It may not turn out exactly as you planned, you know."

"I know that, Mother. But again, that's something that I'll have to deal with when I get there. All I know is that I have a contract to teach there for two years."

Louise was uneasy when she heard this. "Annie, two years is a long time," she said. "You might get tired of it before then."

"Don't worry about it, Mom." Anna was beginning to sound defiant. "Like I said, that's a bridge I'll cross when I come to it."

"Well, if it works out that you don't like it there, don't hesitate to come home," Louise said, sympathy dripping from her words.

Anna shrugged. "The worst thing they could do would be to fire me, and that way I wouldn't have a choice."

That was the worst thing they could do? Anna wondered as she lay on her bed. Was this really the worst that could happen, or was there more to this whole ordeal than met the eye? It was all plain and simple, yet complicated at the same time. A professor at twenty-three? That really did sound too good to be true. Perhaps her mother was right. Perhaps this was a bit more than Anna could handle. The more she thought about it, the more Anna began to regret her decision to come here in the first place. But it was too late to turn back now.

After meditating a while in her semi-naked state, Anna got up, put on a long blue robe, and stepped out onto the terrace next to her room. It was early evening now, and Anna could see the lights of the city from the balcony. She folded her hands as she leaned against the iron rail.

What will this year be like? she wondered. Really, what would it be like?

The next day Anna went in for her job. She was going to a place she had never seen before, working for somebody she had never met before, and doing work she had never done before. These were already bad odds. Little did Anna know that this would be where the problems only started.

Anna's interview was not until early afternoon. But since she had awakened rather early that morning, she decided to take a stroll around the city to see what it was like. So before going directly to the interview, Anna got dressed and went outside.

Anna's hotel was right along the main avenue. This was the center of town and considered to be the best and richest section. The street itself was lined with trees that stayed green all year. (There was no fall and very little winter in Tunis.) Spending the night there was a good way to "ease into" the lifestyle of Tunis. Everything around the area seemed so modern to her—much like home.

When Anna went outside, it was warm and sunny. Though late September, one could say it was still summertime in Tunis. (The weather was typical of what one might think it might be in a country such as Tunisia.) Once Anna started walking along the main avenue, one of the first things she noticed was that, though there were countless women on the streets, there were almost none in the cafés. Nevertheless, Anna did intend to have coffee somewhere, so she looked around for one of the better cafés, found one, and went inside.

For Anna, one of the "better" cafés meant one that had more of a French atmosphere. The café she had just found had that appeal. It had small round tables with chairs around them, large glass windows facing the street, and waiters who wore black jackets and vests. The Arabic cafés, on the other hand, had only a few wooden tables and chairs and a bar, behind which only a few men served everyone. In the latter type of café, Anna thought she would attract more unwanted attention, since it seemed that a lower class of men frequented these bars—the kind of men who would harass her more. Yet at the café Anna had chosen, none of the men inside acted as if they even noticed her. They looked as if they realized that she was a foreigner and that her habits were different from theirs.

Leaving the café, Anna decided to take a walk up to the famous Souks, where they sold merchandise, and where one could bargain the goods down to almost any price. Reaching the end of the main avenue, she approached the Arc de France, which looked to Anna like nothing more than the remaining archway to an ancient fallen wall that might have encircled the city at one time. From here on, she was no longer in the chic center of town, but was now in the Medina—and this was quite a different story.

The Medina was dirty, dilapidated, and primitive. Though electricity and running water existed in most of the houses, living conditions were atrocious. Most of the houses had no roofs, just open, paved centers with bedrooms surrounding them. Here, the women spent most of the time washing clothes and preparing the food during the day and rarely went outside. The children in this district were obviously from impoverished backgrounds. They were dressed in ragged clothing, and their hair and complexions were noticeably unkempt. They spent most of their time playing in the streets or wandering from the house of one neighbor to another—evidence that they were seriously neglected. Aside from the private homes and the people in them, the public restaurants in the Medina seemed dirty and run-down and would certainly not be places to eat. (These restaurants and cafés were of the kind that Anna would expect to find serving the "lower class" people she had previously noted.) Yet Anna hadn't seen the half of it. The only thing she noticed right away was that there was a marked difference between this area and the center of town.

From the Medina, Anna continued on to the Souks. The Souks were cobblestone alleys that were covered at the top like an archway and which ascended as if they were built on an uplifted plateau. They were very traditional, probably dating back to the Middle Ages. Inside, everything imaginable was sold—anything from clothes to iron goods could be found there. So Anna, feeling curious enough to take a peek, went in and started walking up the alley. As she was browsing around the various stores, she began to notice all the items for the tourists: furniture, pictures, toy camels, etc. This led her to believe that Tunisia was basically a tourist country. This proved indeed to be an understatement.

Tunisia, a poor country, depended more on the economy of other countries than it did on its own. Any of its supposed wealth was put up as a front for the tourists. The country itself had a very modern and progressive appearance, but that was only because this was the way foreigners wanted to see it. At least, this is how Anna saw it for the time being. It was also possible that this was the way she wanted to see it.

As Anna continued walking up the Souks, she was marked right away as a foreigner. She was noticed immediately by the young men selling small tokens and souvenirs. There was no doubt in Anna's mind that every one of them wanted her to come into their shop. Yet before she could even think of trying to get away from them, one of them called out to her.

"Come, mademoiselle," he said to her. "Come and see what's in here."

"No," Anna said with a grin. "I don't have any money right now."

"Come in anyway," he begged. "Just have a look at what's in here."

Anna shook her head and kept on walking. Even though he was acting as if he were more interested in making a sale than in making anything else, Anna did not want to get involved. There was something slick and aggressive about this fellow, and she already felt as if she should be wary of people like that.

After a brief look at the Souks, the Medina, and the main avenue, Anna went back to her hotel room and started getting ready for her interview. This time would be about the only time Anna would dress fit to kill. She put on a lace ruffled blouse, a fine linen skirt with a matching jacket, and platform sandals. She wore mounds of foundation and lipstick—which she rarely did—and put on heavy eye makeup, which she never did. She tied her hair up into a nice, neat knot, when usually it was in a loose chignon or ponytail, or just draped across her shoulders. Then she looked at herself in a large mirror on the inside of her door. She approved. Somehow though, Anna felt strangely uncomfortable, as if she were in somebody else's skin. But whose? When she went out for the second time that day, she found out whose.

Again, one could say that women were seen often on the streets of Tunis. In fact, during the day, they were seen as often as men. The older women were quite aged and fat.

Most of them covered themselves with long, white veils which looked more like bed sheets to Anna than anything else. The younger women, on the other hand, were quite pretty. They had a Mediterranean type of beauty. Their faces were round and soft. Many of them had hazel eyes that were warm and glowing, complementing their dark complexions. They had voluptuous figures, too. Although short-legged, their breasts and hips were in good proportion to the rest of their body. They were, in a sense, very attractive. But Anna took a good look at them again and suddenly thought of the image of herself she'd seen in the mirror before she left her room. That's not me, that's them, she thought.

It was true. Almost all of the young Tunisian women she saw that day were heavily made up; almost all were well-dressed and had every hair in place. To Anna, they looked more like models or mannequins than human beings, and this superficial type of beauty, she actually detested. Yet this was not the full extent of it. The more Anna saw of this artificiality, the more uncomfortable she felt herself. That's not me, that's them, she repeated. At any rate, she couldn't wait to go home and change.

An interview is an interview, and one must always be careful with future employers, so Anna was already nervous about this so-called interview. So she walked hurriedly to find the address she wanted. When she arrived at the building she was looking for, she looked around for another possible entrance. This "university" was not one-fifth the size of a high school in the United States. It looked more to Anna like a dinky office building. She stood there and stared at it. She was disappointed, or perhaps a better word would be stunned. But again, good, bad, or indifferent, this was the place. So she went in.

From the first time that she set foot inside the Institute, Anna knew that she didn't belong there. A feeling of coldness and indifference swept over her. Yet she still did not know the worst of it. For every time that she would go into the building from this time on, the feeling would only get worse. At this moment Anna couldn't put her finger on it, but she knew that this wasn't going to work. She would find out why later.

When she went in, Anna seemed to be noticed right away. She didn't know why everybody was staring at her, but she did not take it as a compliment. Still, even though she was already beginning to feel self-conscious, she tried to ignore the feeling as much as possible. So instead of responding to this undue attention, she simply went up to the front desk.

"I would like to see the director," she said quietly, trying not to attract any more attention.

The young man at the desk made an effort to be formal. "Third floor," he said abruptly. His eyes followed Anna curiously as she went over to the stairs and walked up.

Arriving at the third floor, Anna went directly to the secretary's office. "I would like to see the director," she repeated, imitating the formality she had previously encountered. "I have an appointment to see him."

"An appointment?" the secretary replied coldly. "We don't have fixed appointments here."

Anna couldn't believe what she had just heard. For God's sake, she thought. She had come six thousand miles for this interview. The least they could do would be to accept the rendezvous beforehand. "I wrote to the director telling him I would be here at this time," she said defensively. "He should be expecting me now."

"I'm sorry," the secretary retorted. "But the only thing you can do is sit and wait for him to see you."

Needless to say, Anna was already put off by this cold detachment. But she had not seen anything yet. She had not yet met the director. Finally, she did get to see him, after he called his secretary on the phone to let her in.

When Anna entered the director's office, which was right next door, she saw that it was about three times the size of the secretary's office, where often two women worked. His was renovated—theirs wasn't. His had upholstered furniture and even a coffee table—theirs had only desks and chairs. His was big enough inside to be able to entertain—theirs had hardly enough space in which to work. Seeing this, Anna thought that the least he could have done was give them a little room to breathe.

The director was terribly polite. He stood up as Anna entered the room and then reached briskly for her hand. But once that was over, he plopped back into his swivel chair and started turning a bit. "Miss Daleddo," he addressed her, again in the same formal tone, "what brings you here to see me?"

Anna was ready to walk out that minute. "Don't you remember that you sent me a contract to teach here during the next two years?" she reminded him. "I wrote back to you telling you that I was coming to Tunis to see you." Then she sat down in front of him.

"Oh, yes." The director was a little embarrassed about his apparent negligence but still kept a cool demeanor. "I'm sorry," he responded, "but I've been involved with a few other things at the moment. So I temporarily set the incoming contracts aside and am presently working on the curricula for this coming year."

Anna's tough luck. Oh, well, she thought. She figured she might as well get down to business, in spite of the fact that the director had completely forgotten about her. "I was wondering if we could go over the conditions of the contract together before I sign it."

The director pondered for a few seconds, then suddenly snapped out of his state of contemplation. It almost seemed as if his mind were a thousand miles away from what they were discussing right then. "Oh, of course," he said. "May I see your copy?"

Anna sighed disgustedly as she pulled her copy of the contract out of her purse and put it on the director's desk. "Here it is," she told him.

Once the director had put on his reading glasses, he reluctantly leaned forward and picked up the contract from his desk. He looked it over inattentively and then looked back at Anna. "What is it you want me to help you with?" he inquired coldly.

The more time she spent with this man, the more Anna began to realize that she was wasting her time. "I was wondering if we were in agreement with everything stated in the contract," she explained.

The director raised his eyes as he looked over the contract one more time. "Why, of course," he said decisively. "That is, if you are in agreement with everything."

Anna didn't know what else to say. She realized she was going nowhere fast. But she still was not about to pass up the opportunity to talk to the director, now that she was there. "I wanted to know a little more about the last clause," she said. "That's the one about termination."

This was a perfect opportunity for the director to intimidate Anna for the very first time. "Miss Daleddo," he said, still looking down at the contract, "all this says is that if you prove to be professionally incompetent, you can be terminated at any time."

Oh, dear, Anna thought. What the director was saying was that she could be fired without a moment's notice. Well, at least she had found this out early, so hopefully, she wouldn't go into the job with any illusions. Nevertheless, she did not at all like the director's attitude about this whole meeting. He seemed completely indifferent about Anna's position there—until they got to a negative aspect of it. Then it seemed as if he was dying to back her into a corner and scare the living daylights out of her. It was a cinch for Anna to figure out that her new boss was going to be extremely demanding or even an absolute perfectionist.

What Anna did not realize was that this would indeed turn out to be an understatement.

"I guess that's all I really needed to know," Anna said meekly. "So I suppose I am ready to sign the contract now." With an almost sadistic smile on his face, the director handed Anna a pen. Reluctantly, she took it and signed her name on the last page of the contract. Even though this is what she had planned to do all along, somehow Anna felt as if she were signing away her whole individuality. She felt as if she were sacrificing her entire personality and character for this job. Now Anna was sure that she would be nothing more than a servant to this man. However, signing the contract is what she had planned to do, so that is what she did.

"Here it is," she said, as she handed the contract back to the director.

"Very good," he affirmed. "So now it is official that you will be teaching here." Again, there was something hard and intimidating in the director's voice.

"Yes," Anna agreed. I guess that's the way it works, she rationalized to herself.

Anna saw no reason to stay there any longer. She didn't want to, anyway. She already felt dejected enough. So as soon as Anna got up from her seat, so did the director. Then he led her to the door.

"Goodbye, Miss Daleddo," he said, shaking her hand again.

"Goodbye," she replied. Then she walked out.

Needless to say, Anna felt as if she had accomplished little that day. It was obvious that the director was preoccupied with other, more crucial matters. Though there was one thing Anna could truthfully say about the director. In many ways he was a very impressive person. Besides being a not bad looking man—tall and trim—his English was immaculate. With him, Anna had no need to speak French. The "Dr." before his name implied that he had a Ph.D. and that he had obtained his degree in the United States. He could not have been much more than forty years of age, which was quite young to have such a high position—but he was not alone. In countries like Tunisia, men any older than this were lucky to know how to read or write.

Once the interview was finished and Anna had left the director's office, she thought about it. What an arrogant, yet insecure person, she thought to herself. If only he knew how obvious a façade it was—and with somebody who had so much to offer.

Chapter 2

Fall vacation in New York was soon over, and the Daleddo family was back in the suburbs of Baltimore, with of course the exception of Anna. They lived in an upper-class, but nouveau-riche neighborhood. That is to say, most of the people who lived there were uneducated yet financially successful and had gaudy tastes. The Daleddos were one of the few exceptions.

Robert, a physics major, was now an engineer, and Louise had a master's degree in English. Though by no means aristocrats, they showed a certain amount of sophistication in their surroundings. Their house was English Tudor, with stone on the outside and mahogany paneling on the inside. The hardwood floors were covered with Oriental rugs, and the walls were complemented with oil paintings. As Robert had traveled in Europe, Africa, and the Orient, he had brought back antiques and furniture from many different countries. They were not terribly conservative in their decorating, but they were not flashy, either.

Nevertheless, looking at the area as a whole, one could gain an entirely different impression. Judging from the Cadillacs, swimming pools, condominiums, and vacations abroad, it was safe to say that the residents of this neighborhood were very materialistic. While Anna considered all this as "their business," Paul was far more influenced by this superficiality. While Anna would try to find satisfaction in "the finer things in life," Paul would strive for ultimate wealth and success. While Anna would say, "Money doesn't always make you happy," Paul would say "Yeah, they're crying their way to the bank." Neither of them knew that they were right.

Paul wanted, at any cost, to be successful, to make money, to live well. In themselves, these were not unreasonable goals for a young man of 26, but goals can become obsessions, and this was the case for Paul. He had a fantastic job, and it was this that posed the problem. He was a computer salesman. So it was his responsibility to understand computers inside and out in order to be able to sell them. But he didn't. Paul's sales ability was passable, but his understanding of highly complicated hardware was almost nonexistent. Even more difficult for Paul was that in the field of computer sales, he was the low man. This meant that he would be obligated to go out and look for potential customers on his own, with no help from his employers or colleagues.

As planned, Paul would soon be moving down to North Carolina. Conveniently enough, his new job was about a twenty-minute ride from his new house, which he had bought less than a month ago. On the contract for the house, he had collaborated with an elderly aunt, or really, a great aunt—an aunt of his mother's. Addabelle, or "Addie," as her family called her, was over 70 years of age and was 50 percent blind, but she possessed a good sense of humor. She always walked with a sensor cane—glaucoma had afflicted her twenty years before, leaving her eyesight severely damaged. Still, she worked in a factory right up to retirement age and now had a good pension. A few months before, she'd had a chance to buy, in a small town, an old mansion that had been abandoned by its previous owners. At one time, the house had belonged to one of the richest families in the country, but now the neighborhood had gone downhill and so had the value of the house.

Even so, Addie was set on buying this house for the fantastically low price of $40 thousand. The problem was that she was too old to sign alone. She needed a cosigner, and that is where Paul came in. Paul was young, single, and had no legal responsibilities. He also didn't have a house of his own. So what could be more perfect? Addie, a basically principled person, had good intentions. She wanted to help Paul as much as herself. The plan, however, was full of loopholes.

For one thing, there was the problem of the neighborhood and declining property values. Even security was a problem. It was downright dangerous to live there alone, especially for a woman of Addie's age. Second, there was the question of renovation and furnishing. Though it had a strong and sturdy frame, the house was in terrible condition on the inside, and with some twenty rooms, it would take an enormous amount of time and money for it to realize its potential. And finally, the man who sold them the house was an unscrupulous crook. He left out anything that would not be a benefit to him, such as insurance or equity on the house. All he cared about was the money he was getting on the deal.

It was often a question to everyone as to why Paul and Addie would want such a large house for just the two of them. The answer was quite simple. They wanted it mostly for the status and prestige of owning a mansion. Addie, having been brought up during the Depression, came from one of the most prominent families in the area at the time. Paul, on the other hand, had been raised in an environment where everybody was affluent. Nevertheless, they both had something to prove to themselves and to everybody else. They wanted to prove that they still had it in them to afford an impressive place to live.

Yet Paul and Addie had virtually no foresight as to what dilemmas this new undertaking would bring about. Addie, being an elderly woman, did not even think of the actual danger of living in the house. She rationalized that she would be protected by her nephew's presence there, but it never crossed her mind that he might not be there for as long as she would be. She never suspected that Paul might have to leave that house for one reason or another. Paul, as well, did not think of the financial pressures of owning such an estate at his age. He also did not take into consideration the fact that Addie might not live that much longer, leaving him with the responsibility of paying for the rest of the mortgage on his own. Finally, neither of them thought of the unnerving effect that living under the same roof for any pro-longed period of time might have.

Given this neglect of insight, Paul and Addie were nothing short of ecstatic about this new arrangement. They could hardly wait to settle the sale of the house and move in. A date for this would be set up shortly. Until that time, how-ever, Paul could not help but show his eager enthusiasm. When at home, all Paul ever talked about was "the house"— how they didn't make houses like they used to, what fine quality it was, and how close it would be to his job. He could find no fault or pitfalls to this deal. His parents humored him, saying that what he was doing would open fantastic doors for the future (which at the time was true). When his sister was there, she said nothing for or against the idea. On the surface, she appeared to be quite neutral about the matter. His friends, on the other hand, seemed somewhat threatened and jealous about such an opportunity. They were also quite materialistic and competitive. So by this point, it was a question of their outdoing Paul, or vice versa.

A perfect example of Paul's indiscreet relationship with his comrades displayed itself not long before Paul bought his house. One evening, when a friend of his was at the Daleddo's house with his fiancee, all they seemed to want to do was flash her engagement ring under every-body's nose. Anna was a bit disgusted and tried to ignore the whole scene. Later, however, once the guests had gone, her brother offered another point of view. Paul, who didn't even have a girlfriend—much less a fiancée—asked his father where he could pick up a cheap diamond. That was absolutely the last straw. Anna did say something to her mother regarding Paul's growing fanaticism. And Louise was in total agreement.

Paul was already packing up his belongings to move to North Carolina. Among the things he couldn't decide whether to take or leave were his guide manuals from Steamers' Inc., the company he had previously worked for. They had been issued to him when he started there. These hardbound volumes stood on his shelves like an encyclopedia, yet they just collected dust.

Paul did not even understand the language and terms used. It was all computerized knowledge that took almost an engineer to relate to.

While looking through these books, Paul reminisced about what a good time he'd had when he was at Steamers.' All he had seemed to do was go out for lunch and coffee all day. He was never there, not because he didn't want to work, but because he didn't know how to. With this new job, however, Paul told himself that all this would change. This time, he thought, things would be different.

Finally, the day came when Paul and Addie would sign on the dotted line. Louise was extremely tense about the whole affair. She knew that her aunt was headstrong and her son naive. She tried to emphasize that health problems could cause possible limitations to Addie. She attempted to warn Paul about the debt he was putting himself into. But it didn't change anything. Their minds were made up. They would sign.

Once done, Paul and Addie rented a huge van and moved to Greensboro, North Carolina, where most of Louise's family lived. (The house was, in fact, about five minutes' distance from Bobby, Louise's brother, and his family.) Louise's side of the family, though basically dynamic and conscientious, were much more slow-moving and easygoing than Robert's relatives. They were intelligent people who kept up with themselves and nobody else. For this reason, Paul felt much more comfortable with them than he did with his paternal relatives. He also felt less threatened by them. For these people were typical of those who came from the southern part of the U.S.—and would surely never accomplish what his other cousins would.

Having driven all night, Paul and Addie arrived there early the next morning. When they got to Greensboro, they were so excited about their coming plans that they started moving in right away. Exhausted, yet numb, they worked for hours without stopping, until almost everything was well arranged. Finally, in the afternoon, they took a break to eat something. They both went into the huge, antique-style kitchen, sat down at the table, and started eating a "picnic" lunch they had brought with them in the van. Not saying anything to Paul, Addie sat back in her chair and began to fantasize about the time when the house must have been built. She dreamed about living in that era again. Then she thought about her own life.

Addie had been born and reared in North Carolina. Aside from being headstrong, she was extremely individualistic. She never married and never missed it. During the Depression, she supported herself and her mother, who was suffering from a stroke. When Louise's father died, she took in all of her sister's children, one after the other, until Louise's mother remarried. When everybody grew up and left her, she carried on as if nothing had changed. She had many interests—reading, painting, sewing—most of which she did with the aid of a magnifying glass.

At the same time, though, Addie had many strange habits. She had no sense of order. Housework was not one of her basic interests. She had magazines that dated back ten years, not because she was a collector, but because she had forgotten to throw them away. She was also a cat lover. Her two black pets ran and hid any time anybody (except Addie) came around. She adored gambling and had lost a lot of money that way. Paul always knew that Addie was a good and decent person, but he would soon find out that living with her was another story.

Like Anna, Paul was beginning his new job right away. Between moving and getting ready to start work, he hardly had time to catch his breath. But the next day he was off and running. Unlike Anna, though, Paul was always well dressed, wearing expensive-looking suits, shirts, and ties. There was a conservative but stylish look about him. His hair was never too long or short, and he always had a tasteful flair in his dressing. But Paul still had the basic good looks of Anna and, for that matter, their parents. Though not tall, he had a broad and well-proportioned physique. He paid special attention to his diet and worked out regularly at a health spa. As a result, his weight rarely fluctuated. His eyes were hazel, his complexion clear, and his hair thick and brown.

He was almost late that morning. Quickly, he parked and hurried out of his car, taking his attaché case with him. As always, Paul looked professional and "zippy," along with it. So, taking care to maintain his appropriate appearance, Paul walked primly into the huge office building marked "Mackenfield" in big letters on the outside. (It was an international company, and they let everybody know it.)

The inside of the building reminded Paul very much of Steamers, Inc. It was all new and modern. All along the main floor were business offices with computers galore. For Paul, just entering one of these rooms was practically devastating. The noise and commotion of the countless machines and the people working on them was enough to shock anybody. It was exactly this that seemed to be the main difference between Steamers and Mackenfield—the size of the offices and the amount of activity found within them. At Steamers, many offices were small, and some rooms even contained several offices. At Mackenfield, however, the business offices were enormous and were therefore found on the lower floors, while the executive suites were five flights up.

Seeing this scared Paul already, making him wish that he were still back with his previous company. He recognized right away that this job was going to be considerably more challenging than his other position, and it was precisely this that frightened him. Deep inside, Paul knew that if he hadn't been able to make headway at his other job, it would be even more difficult for him to succeed at this new one. What was he going to do this time? Paul was already worried sick. Oh, well, he finally concluded. He figured that he would have to play it by ear.

So after taking a quick peek at the technical equipment and services they had there, Paul took the elevator up to the fifth floor. When the door opened, he walked out and down the hall. Here Paul saw nothing but closed doors marked at the top with various names. Eventually, he found the door he wanted. Written on it was the name "Milsten"—the person Paul would be working for. He opened the door quietly, finding a modern, decorated, carpeted office with a pretty secretary sitting at the main desk.

"Hello," she said cordially. "You must be the new boy."

Paul really didn't know how to react to that comment, so he answered her. "Yes," he replied timidly. "I'm Paul Daleddo."

"Please, let me show you to your office," she told him. "You can start moving your things in whenever you like. Mr. Milsten will see you when he has time."

The secretary was so polite, so friendly, so terribly charming, that she made Paul feel much more comfortable. He thought he might begin to be at ease here after all. However, when he entered his new office, that cold and nervous feeling came over him again.

It was literally cool in his office. The heat hadn't been on in some time, and the door was always closed. Nevertheless, the office, besides being immaculately clean, was typical of that of a successful businessman. Carpeted, it had a mahogany desk with a high-back swivel chair. Though there were no coffee tables in this office, Paul had enough space so he could decorate as he wished, and he also found several sets of bookshelves against the wall.

So much room! What would he do with it all? Presumably, the secretary thought that Paul had books and documents in his car to move into his new office. He had nothing. Paul had decided not even to take his manuals from Steamers with him. All he had now were a few leaflets and papers the new company had given him. These were in his attaché case. There was no need to rearrange them.

Paul went over to his desk and sat down in the swivel chair behind it. He sat there for a while, turning the chair from side to side. Then he reached into his pocket and pulled out a pack of cigarettes, along with a fancy gold lighter. After he lit up, he tossed the cigarettes and lighter onto the desk. For a while, he puffed away, still turning in his chair. In a way, Paul felt as if he were a big shot—but in another way, he didn't. His ego felt sky high in this new environment, yet somehow, he felt empty inside. In the back of his mind, he probably realized even then that things would fall to the ground soon enough.

Paul had smoked three cigarettes, filling up the ashtray on the desk—which was also marked "Mackenfield." About an hour had passed, and no one had arrived yet. It soon crossed Paul's mind that Mr. Milsten didn't care whether this new employee of his lived or died. Paul knew that the man must be busy, but making him wait this long was out-of-line. After all, Paul's time was valuable, too.

After waiting a while longer, Paul finally decided to go out somewhere for coffee. Not wanting to miss Milsten, he elected to go to a cafeteria-style restaurant across the street.

So quickly, he went over to the restaurant and ordered a large cup of coffee to go. Feeling rather rushed, he finished half of it inside the cafeteria and then took the other half with him back to the office.

When he got there, he stayed alone for at least another half hour. The more he found that he had to wait for this man, the more annoyed Paul began to feel regarding this lack of consideration. How would Milsten feel if it were turned the other way around? He wouldn't tolerate this kind of nonsense in a million years, Paul was sure of it.

But finally, Milsten did come in to see him. When he saw that Paul was already there, however, he looked surprised. Nevertheless, he gave him a friendly smile and closed the door quietly. He went over to the desk and greeted Paul with a warm handshake. Then they both sat down.

Milsten was a man of about fifty, bald and overweight. His face had a reddish tinge to it, probably from too much drinking. Even so, he seemed to be rather zippy himself, clad in a tweed suit, colorful shirt, and silk tie. Like his secretary, Milsten appeared to be a very pleasant, amiable person who was obviously conscious of good public relations.

Paul expected some long discourse, but Milsten started out by simply looking around the bare room. "Haven't you moved any of your things in?" He sounded almost confused.

This obviously made Paul feel uncomfortable and embarrassed. "Oh, I have a few things at my house," he rationalized. "I'll move them in when I have time."

Then his boss looked at the empty coffee cup and the ashtray full of butts. When he has time? the boss questioned in his mind. What does he have now? Now Milsten was even more confused. He really didn't understand where Paul was coming from.

"I understand that you've signed the contract and are ready to start," he addressed Paul.

"Yes, I have," Paul confirmed. "I mailed it to your secretary about a week ago."

"So now I guess we can tie up some loose ends." Milsten sounded quite casual.

"Yes," Paul said quietly. "I guess so."

There was nothing intimidating about Milsten's personality—nothing hard or severe and nothing demanding. On the contrary, he seemed to Paul to be almost too easygoing, too ambiguous. In fact, as far as he was concerned, Milsten acted as if he really didn't give a damn. Milsten turned out to be exactly the type of person Paul had feared he would be.

"Have you taken a look at some of our latest models?" Milsten was referring to the computers on the ground floor.

"Yes, I saw them before I came up to the office. That's quite a selection you have there." Paul acted so impressed by what he had seen earlier that he actually sounded scared.

"As you know, it is your job to sell them," Milsten smiled. It was almost as if he were joking.

"Yes, I know." Paul remained serious at any cost. Now he was so nervous that he was sitting up straight in his chair. "But where do I get the leads?"

"Oh, there are companies and businesses all over that need computers. It's the going thing. You'll find people who are interested in buying." Milsten still sounded nonchalant.

"Yes, but doesn't the secretary have names of potential clients?" This time it was Paul who was a bit confused.

Milsten sat back in his chair, looking a bit concerned, but still not uneasy. He raised his eyebrows and took a deep breath. "I'm afraid that if you try leads, you'll always be too late," he explained. "You see, there are three other men in this office who have been here for quite a while. They get first pick."

When he heard this, Paul did well to hide his despair. But how could he get angry? Milsten was only saying what was true. Besides, that's the way it ought to be. He certainly couldn't deny that Milsten was being totally open, fair, and honest about everything. As far as Paul was concerned, though, he realized that he was completely done for, before he even started.

Milsten glanced at his watch and then looked up at Paul. "I'm sorry, but I'm having lunch with some business associates. We're meeting at Simon's for cocktails at eleven-thirty. I really must go," he apologized. "But feel free to talk to your colleagues or secretary. I'm sure they'll be happy to help you." He smiled again as he got up to leave.

Paul stood up with Milsten and showed him to the door. With his usual cordiality, Milsten shook his hand and wished Paul "good luck." Then he walked out. After closing the door slowly, Paul walked listlessly back to his swivel chair. He plopped into it and started turning again. Then he thought about it some more.

How could he ever get any leads if the others had first pick? It would be the same thing all over again. Could he at least make a go of it this time? He doubted it. Now Paul was getting pensive. He felt he had to leave this environment before it surrounded him on all sides and squelched him completely. He realized that in any shape, form or fashion, he just had to get out.

Not knowing what else to do, Paul went out to lunch.

Chapter 3

Less than two weeks later, Paul and Addie had their house completely arranged. Though most of the rooms were quite bare, they had managed to make the library rather elegant. Addie had an Oriental rug from her old house and a few antiques that had been handed down in her family. There was also a fireplace in the library that Paul had done a good job of reconstructing. Now they made use of it almost every night, since with a house that size, and gas heat at a premium, they would have been foolish not to. The leaves were turning, and cold weather was already in the air, but Paul and Addie were quite cozy and comfortable in their new home. They both relaxed, Addie in her rocking chair and Paul on the sofa, sitting in front of the fire together.

"You know," Addie mentioned. "When I was young, this was the only heat in the house."

"Oh, really?" Paul wasn't listening.

"My father would chop up the wood in the back yard and bring it in," she continued. "He would build a fire that always smoldered by the time we went to bed. But it didn't matter. The cats were in bed with us. We were never cold." Addie gave a low chuckle.

Then lo and behold, one of the cats came in and curled up in front of the fire. Paul didn't notice that either. He was still daydreaming. He was still fantasizing about how things should have gone at work. He was thinking about the kind of progress he should have been making at his new job.

During the daytime, Paul didn't seem to get much accomplished. In a way, it was like his old job—in a way, it wasn't. At least at Steamers, he had the company of another young salesman who wasn't performing. They were both, in fact, "asked to quit" their previous job. But now Paul was completely alone. His colleagues were all at least ten years older than he was, and his secretary was unfortunately married. He had no one there to stimulate him during his free time, which was most of the time.

Paul had already thought of changing jobs, but he was sure that the exact same thing would happen all over again. He would only start a vicious cycle of distress and dissatisfaction. He had also thought of quitting this type of work altogether, but to him that would be like giving up. As far as Paul was concerned, leaving this job would mean that he was a complete and utter failure. He had to hang on to it, no matter what the outcome would be. This time around, he had to keep the job.

The next day Paul went to work as usual. When he went in, he found two men from another company talking to one of his colleagues. Apparently, they were interested in buying a computer for their business. Before going into his office, Paul overheard the men conversing. They were saying that the computer was too expensive and that it wasn't efficient enough for its price. They appeared to be driving a hard bargain with Barley, Paul's colleague. However, when Paul went into his office and came out five minutes later, he saw that the three of them looked quite content. The two businessmen shook hands with Barley and left the office. Meanwhile, Barley was still standing there, smiling from ear to ear.

"Who were those two guys?" Paul asked.

"They were from Denton Steel," Barley told him, still grinning. "I just sold them a computer for twenty grand. They tried to bid lower, but I wouldn't budge."

"Denton?" Paul replied. "That's one of the biggest steel producers in the country. How did you manage that?" He was obviously green with envy.

"The secretary gave me their name."

The secretary gave him their name. Meanwhile, Paul was supposed to go out knocking on doors looking for clients. Paul didn't dare go to the secretary for leads like that. For one thing, he knew that he would always be the last one to get the name, and for another, he was too afraid of appearing aggressive. Being so young and so new here, Paul was in a very insecure position. He realized that at any time, he could be pushed down and out by somebody else in the office. This was the very reason that Paul was so afraid of coming off as a threat to any one of his colleagues or to Milsten. He feared that if he offered them enough competition or rivalry for the names and sales leads, they might offer him a good opportunity to get lost, once and for all.

But a few days later, Paul finally made up his mind that he was going to at least try to make a sale somewhere. So he went to the restaurant where he usually got his coffee. When he went in, he was recognized right away as a regular customer. Paul approached the cashier reluctantly with an unexpected request.

"I'd like to see the manager," he said shyly.

The cashier looked surprised but responded by saying, "I'll see if he's in his office right now."

Then she went through the main door of the kitchen, that apparently led to the manager's office. Meanwhile, Paul waited next to the cash register. When the cashier returned a few minutes later, she was still alone.

"He'll see you when he has time," she told him. "Why don't you have a seat at one of the tables while you wait for him?"

With that suggestion, Paul decided to take the cashier up on her offer. So after he had gotten himself a cup of coffee, he sat down at one of the tables as he waited for the manager to come and see him. As always, this process took a while—the manager must have had many more important matters to take care of. But finally, he did come out to talk to Paul.

"Hi," he greeted him as he walked up to the table. "What can I do for you?"

When the manager came up to him, Paul stood up and shook his hand in a rather formal fashion. "My name is Paul Daleddo," he said, clearing his throat. "I am from the Greensboro branch of Mackenfield. My office is across the street."

"Oh, really?" The manager acted rather disinterested. He was evidently in a hurry and anxious for Paul to get to the point.

"Yes," Paul replied. "I was sort of wondering if you would be interested in buying a computer from my company for your company."

When he heard this, the manager almost laughed out loud. The boy is trying to make a sale, he thought. It was obvious to him that Paul lacked experience and polish in doing what he was supposed to be doing right then. Still, the manager tried to be polite about giving him what he considered to be a valid refusal. "I'm sorry, Mr. Daleddo," he apologized. "But this restaurant already has a regular company from which we buy our hardware. Besides, we are not in need of any new models at this time."

As Paul was expecting a response similar to this, he felt neither hurt nor disappointed. What did he expect? The man got his merchandise from somebody who had better leads and connections than he did. For that matter, Paul wondered if it had even been worth a try in the first place. "That's OK," Paul agreed. "I thought I'd ask, that's all."

"I'm glad you did," the manager smiled. "If I'm ever in need of anything that you could sell me, I won't hesitate to contact you at your office."

"That's very kind of you," Paul added, knowing that he would probably never see the man again.

"Thank you for your offer," the manager said, shaking Paul's hand again. "I hope that someday I'll have the opportunity to take you up on it."

"Thank you," Paul reciprocated.

"I'm afraid I have to go now," the manager informed him. "It's nearly lunch time, and I'm wanted in the kitchen now. But I'm sure I'll be talking to you later on."

"Sure," Paul said in a disenchanted voice. "I'll see you later."

"Take care," the manager said, tapping him lightly on the shoulder. Then he walked away.

Not knowing what else to do, Paul sat back down in his chair in front of the table. Had it been worth the feeble attempt he had given it? He knew all along what the outcome would be. Everybody seemed to have first pick at everything, except for him. But how could he do anything about it? To Paul, the situation seemed totally hopeless.

Yet in spite of his perpetual failures, this would be neither the first time nor the last time that he would give it another try. Once, for example, Paul went to a store that sold fabric and sewing utensils. There, the day manager told him to come back later when the general supervisor was in. He went there twice, but the supervisor was never there. As before, when he finally did get a chance to see him, the supervisor gave him a flat "no." They got their computers from another company and already had a regular representative from that division.

Obviously, the circumstances were as Paul had seen them all along. Every other company had other representatives who were higher up than he was, and therefore they had first choice. It was as if Paul was being pushed to the back anywhere he went. So no matter what he did, it would inevitably lead to feelings of frustration and defeat for him.

Later that afternoon Paul went down to the computer rooms to see what was there. He went into one of the rooms that had some of the bigger models. There he saw a technician who was "talking" to one of the computers. The technician was feeding it information that the machine would retain and then compute. Eventually, the answer would come out on the monitor screen. Paul found that merely being around these devices was nerve-racking. The ticking of the computers, the messages on the screen, the papers being fed into and out of the machines, overwhelmed Paul, making him feel as if he were in some other, inhuman world. Paul did not understand or appreciate computers and, in fact, he had no desire to. In short, Paul was against the whole computer trend, in spite of his professional responsibilities and commitments to it.

Paul went up to the technician to see what he was doing. He was a young fellow, dressed in a simple striped shirt and faded blue jeans. When he saw that Paul was there, he turned to him and made a brief comment. "How do you like this baby?" he said. "She can really think for herself."

Then Paul approached the machine and looked at it more closely. On the screen it was now reading a single word: "REJECT." Reject what? Paul wondered. What was the computer rejecting? The whole system? Maybe even the whole world. The technician was right. That computer had a mind of its own. Soon machines like that would be walking, talking, and thinking for themselves. Someday they might replace human beings or even control them. Paul had enough insight to realize that he would not be in agreement with such scientific advancement. So why should he support it? Why should he go out and push something that he didn't believe in, in the first place? Yet in spite of the fact that he wasn't comfortable with computers and everything they symbolized to him, they had become too much a part of his life to be able to escape. For Paul, the comprehension and sales execution of computers had become an obsession too strong to break away from.

Paul went home that night feeling as discouraged as ever. He walked up to the front door and opened it. The cats were in the hallway, but they scurried away the minute Paul stepped inside. Then Paul closed the door quietly behind him. Addie was not downstairs, and Paul did not bother to call her. He threw his jacket and attaché case on the sofa in the library and went into the kitchen.

Naturally, the house was exactly as he had left it that morning. In the library newspapers and magazines were all over the floor. In the kitchen, the breakfast dishes were still on the table. There was no dinner prepared. (Addie only ate sandwiches.) Yet despite how much all of this added to his already profound frustration, Paul didn't have the heart to scold Addie about it. How could he order her to do housework when she could hardly see to walk? So instead, Paul went to the kitchen sink, rolled up his sleeves, and started cleaning up. Facing the sink, he was washing the dishes, when Addie appeared at the door with her cane in her hand.

"I didn't hear you come in, Paul," she said.

Paul almost gasped with fright. He hadn't heard her, either.

"I'm sorry," she said. "I didn't mean to startle you."

"That's OK." He calmed down and kept on working.

"How was work today?" Addie inquired.

"It was fine."

"Find any customers?"

"No."

Addie groped her way into the kitchen, moving her cane along the floor in front of her. She went over and stood next to the sink where Paul was standing. "Paul, is there something wrong?" she asked. "Something you want to tell to tell me about?

"No," he answered, not turning toward her. "Everything's fine."

"Are you sure?" she insisted.

"Yes, I'm sure," he replied, still not looking at her.

Addie hesitated a few seconds but felt she had to say one more thing before she left him alone. "Well, if there's anything I can do, just let me know," she advised, offering him what little support she had of her own.

Then Paul stopped what he was doing and looked at her. "Don't worry about it, Aunt Addie," he said. "There's nothing you can do for me. There's nothing anybody can do." Then he turned away and kept on working.

Don't worry about what? There's nothing anybody can do about what? Addie really was confused. She had seen Paul withdrawn like this for weeks now, but she couldn't figure out why. It was for this reason that she did not know how to react to Paul's state of disillusionment. She thought of calling his parents, but they knew less about him that she did. So what really could she do? She finally elected to think about it for a while. Eventually, she would reach at least a temporary solution. So for now she would dismiss the whole question at hand.

After snapping out of her pensive state, Addie went into the library, took an outdated magazine along with her magnifying glass, and sat in front of the fire.

Paul had never had an active sex life. He was always afraid to get too close to any one girl. While in college, he'd had his own room for the last two years he was there. Still, he rarely invited anybody in to spend the night. When he did have a girlfriend over once in a great while, it was almost always a one-night stand. Even when Paul was out dating, it was not necessarily with promiscuous girls, but always with vain and flashy girls—girls he would never want to settle down with. It seemed almost as if he kept this façade of estrangement between himself and the opposite sex on purpose. It was as if he wanted to avoid as much as possible the physical and emotional contact of sex. What actually was lacking in Paul's life? Was it the desire for intimacy, or the desire for sex itself? No one really knew. Paul was not sure himself.

While in Baltimore, Paul had the habit of frequenting bars and discos where other young people like himself would go and hang out at night. Now, living in North Carolina, Paul soon discovered that there weren't that many places like this to be found. Still, he did manage to find a few dinky nightclubs where he could go from time to time to have a drink or two. Since now, there was no one his age, either where he lived or where he worked, Paul thought that by going out at night he could meet people. In the back of his mind Paul always had the idea that he might be able to start a serious friendship and develop a lasting relationship. By this point, though, all that Paul was trying to do was prove himself. He wanted to show that he was something to somebody. Other than this, Paul could have cared less about an intimate relationship with anybody. So in a sense, he was doing nothing less than kidding himself by playing this masquerade.

On Saturday nights Paul would go out to one of his preferred places, located right outside of Greensboro. It wasn't nearly as big as the ones he was used to at home, but it was at least someplace to go. Though now, when he went out, it wasn't the same as when he had been at home. There, he had a gang of friends he saw at least once a week. He had been doing this for years and really enjoyed their company. But now, when he went anywhere at night, he did so alone—and for lack of anything better to do.

Paul had been going to this nightclub every Saturday night since he had been in Greensboro—about two months by now. It was a relatively conservative, sedate place with corny entertainment, but it was as close to nightlife as he was likely to get in North Carolina. It was here and only here that Paul thought he had half a chance of meeting somebody. Just the same, Paul had not had any luck meeting anyone, of any age, since he had been going there. Tonight, however, he would find to be somewhat different.

Paul was sitting there with a drink in front of him, listening to the old-time music the band was playing, when he noticed a tall, blonde woman hanging around his table. She seemed extremely interested in getting to know him. So naturally, after waiting all this time to pick up a girlfriend, Paul was not exactly down on the idea himself.

"Hi," she said, approaching him rather aggressively. "Are you with anybody?" She had the typical southern drawl that Paul was used to hearing by this time.

"No, I'm alone," he told her. Even though Paul felt rather awkward about inviting her to sit with him, he was not about to turn this opportunity down after waiting so long to get it. "Why don't you have a seat with me?"

The woman, in turn, did not waste any time in accepting his offer. She sat down quickly, moving the chair around on the floor noisily. Then Paul asked her the obvious question.

"Want a drink?"

"Don't mind if I do," she replied curtly. "What's that you got there?"

"A whiskey sour," Paul replied.

"I'll have the same," she decided hastily. That offer, she didn't turn down either.

The waitress soon came, and Paul ordered. His new acquaintance was tall—almost taller than Paul was—and she was slim, with really not much of a figure at all. She also seemed older than Paul, looking to be in her late twenties or early thirties. Her ash-blonde hair was shoulder length and obviously blow-dried into a flip style hairdo. She was quite made up, but not in a hard or cheap way. She just wore a lot of rouge and red lipstick to give her color.

"The band is terrible here, isn't it?" she said, trying to promote some kind of conversation.

"Yeah," Paul responded half-heartedly. He acted somewhat disinterested by such small talk. He wanted more to get to know her as a person. "Do you live around here?" he asked her.

"Yeah, I have an apartment not far from here," she answered briefly.

"So you must work around here."

Yeah, I'm a secretary," she told him, not elaborating. Then she changed the subject. "Hey, what are you doing after you leave here?"

Paul was dumbfounded by this question, as he was not expecting to hear it nearly so soon. "I-I don't know," he stuttered. "Go home, I guess."

"Where do you live?" she questioned eagerly.

"In Greensboro."

"Oh, that's too far, and it's too late," she gasped. "You can spend the night at my place. Then in the morning you can go home. I don't want you to drive home like that."

Then Paul smirked to himself. He was three miles from his house, it was ten o'clock at night, and he was stone sober. Really, where was this girl coming from? If she wanted him to come home with her, all she had to do was invite him. She didn't have to make up such silly excuses. Still, Paul knew what his answer would eventually be. So why prolong the inevitable, he figured. So as soon as they both finished their last drink, they left together.

Before he knew it, Paul found himself in a modern, well-decorated, obviously expensive apartment. She had said she was a secretary, he recalled. He concluded that she must have been in a big firm to be able to live like this. It was about midnight by now. The woman had turned on the stereo and had served them both a martini. Soft music played as they both relaxed. She sat on the sofa next to Paul, propped up her stocking feet on the coffee table, and reached for her drink. Paul was quite tense about this whole situation, as he knew exactly what her eventual expectations were going to be. So as soon as he finished his martini, he asked her for another one. With that request, the girl acted rather agitated, as she was just getting comfortable, but she got up just the same and went over to the liquor cabinet. Paul's eyes followed her curiously as she walked across the room.

Actually, Paul did not find her to be a bad-looking woman. She had that "southern belle" quality. She was fair, with blue eyes and thin—possibly too thin. Her taste in clothing was not quite as up-to-date as was her taste in decorating. Instead of wearing blue jeans like Paul, she was dressed in black satin pants and a bright rose blouse probably made out of silk. She had a rhinestone pendant around her neck, or at least that's what Paul thought it was, and a rather large diamond on her right hand. Again, Paul wondered how she was able to live so well on a secretary's salary.

As time went on, Paul became more and more uptight. In fact, he wondered what he was doing there in the first place. He hardly knew the girl, it was obvious that they didn't really appeal to each other, and he didn't even enjoy being with her. So what the hell was he doing here? Again, it was evident that Paul was trying to prove himself to somebody. But what he was trying to prove, even Paul was not sure of.

Paul had already had three drinks—one at the night-club and two at her place—but he was still longing for another. In the meantime, though, he wanted so much to try to promote a little conversation with his new acquaintance. So he asked her another rather normal question.

"What's your name, by the way?"

"Rose," she replied coldly.

"Oh, Rose," he chuckled. "That's cute. It's like the color of your blouse."

"Yeah, I guess so," she responded, not sounding very amused by Paul's trite sense of humor. She did not seem in the least to be interested in talking. All she seemed interested in was clouding her mind with alcohol and eventually going to bed. Tiring of sitting around so long, she got up to get them both another drink.

Once she had prepared two more martinis at the liquor cabinet, she went over and set them both on the coffee table, where Paul was still sitting. Then she went around and plopped back down on the sofa herself, propping her stocking feet up on the coffee table again.

"After this drink, how about if we hit the sack?" she suggested.

"If you want," Paul agreed. Even though he was disheartened by her apathy, he went along with whatever she said.

So they soon finished their last drink and went into the bedroom. While Paul hesitated, she started undressing right away. He just stood in the doorway and watched her for a few seconds. When she got down to her bra and panties, he turned off the light and started undressing himself. She turned toward him, probably wondering why he had turned off the light so abruptly, but she didn't say anything. Then she was the first to slip into bed. He followed shortly afterward.

It was exactly at this point that the roles in their approaches changed. For the first time that night, she tried to be warm and intimate, but it was now too late. Now it was he who was indifferent. She tried to cuddle up to him, but he was totally unresponsive. He just put his arm around her and lay there. Though he was in no rush, she seemed to be quite eager, but again she didn't say anything. There was one thing, however, that saved Paul. By this time he'd had enough alcohol to be able to feel the effect, and this always helped his lovemaking. So when he felt that he was far enough under the influence, he decided to give it a go. He approached her almost violently, kissing and caressing her entire body. He was obviously pushing himself to be passionate, and it came off as exactly that. The entire act seemed very artificial. It was almost as if he were trying to fake it as much to himself as he was to her. When they finally did make love, it was forced and almost painful for Paul. She sensed it, but accepted it once it was done. Once it was completely over, they separated immediately and both stretched out on either side of the bed. Now they made absolutely no effort to try to touch or communicate with one another. The act was finished, and that was it. So, soon afterward, they both dozed off.

For some reason Paul woke up the next morning around seven, which he rarely did on Sundays. When he got up, his lady friend was still asleep. So, being careful not to wake her, he got dressed and left her apartment, leaving no telltale signs of what had happened the night before.

While Paul was driving home, he thought about it. Rose, he remarked. What a name. He didn't even know her name until he was almost in bed with her. Why didn't it come easier to either of them? Evidently, what he was trying to validate to this woman as well as to himself, as being true and realistic, did not come off that way at all. Was it his fault? Or was it just because he didn't know her? At any rate, it was his fault. It was his fault for trying to copulate with a woman he neither loved nor desired. It was his fault for trying to consummate a relationship overnight. It was his fault for trying to do something that just didn't feel right. If he had only realized that he didn't have to rush into an act like that, he would not have been so depressed this morning. Anyway, it was over now. Once he got back to his house, he would forget that it ever happened.

The sun was low in the sky, facing him, as he drove home.

Chapter 4

Within a week Anna had found an apartment in Tunis. She was lucky, as housing in the city was hard to come by and very expensive. She was also fortunate, because a young Tunisian girl was looking for someone to share with, and it seemed to Anna that they would get along well enough. So a couple of days after meeting the girl, Anna moved in with her.

Anna was excited about her new home, because it was a clean place in a good part of the city on the other side of town, quite far from the Medina and all the thieves and muggers who lived in it. She also felt more secure living with another woman. Another reason Anna was enthusiastic about where she lived was because it was a nice apartment, in good condition on the outside and was already partially furnished with antiques. That provided a good basis upon which Anna could start a new project. When she moved in, it was her intention to finish furnishing the apartment.

Anna was basically a creative person and had a lot of taste and finesse in her decorating. So this project with her new pad was exactly what she needed to interest her and keep her going. She was so eager to start collecting things that she went almost immediately to the Souks to do some shopping. There she found a store that sold oil paintings. When she entered it, she seemed right away to catch the eyes of two young salesmen inside. Meanwhile, a certain painting caught Anna's eye. It was a picture of a tall man fighting a creature that resembled the devil. It reminded her much of Raphael's "Saint George and the Dragon," which she adored. Nevertheless, as far as the actual value of the picture was concerned, Anna knew that it was no priceless original. She realized as well that it was pointless to ask them if it was an original. They would say "Yes" regardless of whether it was or not. Needless to say, Anna was not looking forward to the coming debate, but she knew it would have to take place sooner or later. So she reluctantly approached the two men.

"How much do you want for this painting?" she asked as she looked it over. She tried to sound firm and experienced.

"A hundred dinars," one of them called out.

That was ridiculous. Anna was sure it wasn't an original. "I will pay no more than ninety," she told them, feeling too timid to bid any lower. She was already losing her cool.

"A hundred dinars. That's the price!" the other one affirmed.

"Ninety...five?" Anna suggested sweetly, trying to bargain as best she could.

"No," the first one responded. "A hundred dinars it is."

Both of the boys were pleasant about it, but it was clear that they were not going to budge from that price. It was obvious that Anna was a foreigner, presumably a tourist, and to be taken for that. They also saw that she was very impressed with that painting and that she just had to have it at any price, so they figured they would exploit her to that extent.

Then Anna finally gave in, as they knew she inevitably would do. "All right," she sighed. "A hundred dinars is fine." Anna felt rather foolish about being so weak and pliable but handed over the money over just the same.

They wrapped the painting in brown paper, tied some string around the outside, and presented it to Anna. They were obviously happy about the sale they had just made. As Anna was walking out of the store, they muttered something to each other in Arabic. They said it jokingly, almost mockingly. Anna didn't pay much attention. She was happy with the painting, no matter what the price was. So she just left with it.

One of the reasons Anna was in such a hurry to get her apartment in order was that she was starting work officially in two days, the following Monday. She had spoken with the secretary, the director, and a couple of her colleagues—and that was it. With hardly even a curriculum set up, she was supposed to be ready to teach. Again, these were bad odds for her.

But in spite of the undesirable circumstances under which she was starting her new job, Anna was excited about it. So that morning when she got up, Anna thought eagerly about getting ready for work. She sat on her bed, which faced a large antique mirror on the door of her chest. Then she thought about what she should wear. Pants? She didn't dare. None of the women in Tunis wore pants at that time of year. The linen suit? No way. She wasn't going to look like a mannequin again for anybody. She finally decided on a denim skirt and a white embroidered blouse. She really should have dressed up more, especially since it was the first day, but she felt that nothing would be good to wear if she didn't feel comfortable in it.

By the time she was completely dressed and ready to go, it was about quarter of eight. Even though Anna was extremely curious about starting her work at the Institute, there was something about that place that didn't strike her as being quite right. She had been inside it several times already and felt as if the atmosphere was getting to her more and more every time she went back. She found the secretary and director downright offensive—and her colleagues pleasant, but shallow. She didn't really appreciate anybody there. Still, Anna was determined to give it all she had to give for as long as she would be working there. So without any more hesitation, she left her apartment to go to the Institute that Monday morning.

When she got there, Anna found that it was complete madhouse inside. During the first half hour of classes, there were more students in the hall than in the classrooms. When Anna finally did get her class together, she did not even know how to introduce herself. She then made her first big mistake. She let them know her first name. From then on, they would be calling her "Anna" more often than "Miss Daleddo," and later on, this would not go over well at all with the administration.

When Anna started her class and began to converse with some of her students, she was surprised to find that they didn't seem at all to be what she had heard they were like. While Anna had been told that they were often immature, boisterous, and even insolent, they came off to her as being more shy and reserved. They were all dressed conservatively but tastefully—the girls in skirts and dresses and the boys in brand-new pants and slacks. They also seemed to exude a lot of finesse and sophistication in their conduct and mannerisms. The problem was, however, that theirs was a conversation class—and nobody wanted to participate. Though most of the students' English was fairly good, they didn't seem to want to speak it, probably because they were either timid or self-conscious. Every time Anna asked them a question, they would answer briefly and have nothing more to say. They didn't make the least amount of effort to converse with her or with each other. So, feeling very awkward and not knowing what else to do, Anna decided to take the floor and talk about anything that came to her mind. This definitely seemed to arouse the interest of the class. By this time, however, the class was just about over.

The next day things started looking up, or so Anna thought. She was actually under the impression that what she had done the day before had paid off and that now the students were becoming more enthusiastic about her conversation class. The problem was that this conversation was personal to Anna. They would ask her such questions as, "How old are you?" "Do you miss your family?" and "Are you going to marry a Tunisian man?" And Anna would answer them to the best of her knowledge. This was her next big mistake. She was establishing an undesirable relationship with her students that would be impossible to reverse later on.

The positive side of this predicament was that the students seemed to like Anna very much. Like everybody else who knew her, they found Anna to be extremely responsive and personable. Yet in spite of their growing attraction to her, Anna realized that it was wrong to be this kind and friendly to them, as she was well aware of what its later consequences would be. She had been warned by other teachers and associates against this type of interaction with students. No matter how much she tried to keep her distance from them, though, she couldn't help but let her own personality come through. It was too natural—and too difficult for her to change. So as an alternative to putting on such phony airs of sternness and rigidity, Anna merely elected to be herself. It was only in this way that she felt that she would be able to reach her students.

After work each day, Anna had gotten into the habit of going to a nearby restaurant for lunch. It had an open terrace and garden and was also inexpensive. Although the food there was mediocre, Anna found the atmosphere very relaxing. So now she went there regularly.

One day when it was warm out, there were so many people outside that the customers were forced to share tables. So when she finally did get a seat, she found herself face to face with a gentleman about her age. He didn't strike her as particularly handsome. He was swarthy, with rather course features. He had wavy hair and a thick beard that shaped his thin face, and very large, brown eyes. He was of about average height but quite slim. Unlike most of the men she had met there, he appeared rather quiet and uncommunicative. In a way, Anna felt like talking to him. She had seen him in this restaurant several times before and just wanted to get to know him.

She looked up at him as she was eating her meal. "The food isn't very good here," she commented.

He gave Anna a look of surprise. He seemed happy she had made the first move. "No, it isn't," he said, smiling, "but at least it's not expensive."

"That's true."

"Are you French?"

"No, I'm American," she replied. "I assume you're Tunisian."

"Yes."

"Are you a student here?"

"No, I'm a teacher. I teach English at the Institute across the street."

Trying to change the banal routine, he offered Anna something to drink. She then looked at the carafe full of water sitting on the table and politely declined. "No, thank you. I'm fine with this."

Once he had finished his meal, he got up to leave. Then he bade Anna a cordial "au revoir" and walked away. Anna really didn't think that much about it afterward. A nice enough fellow, she concluded.

It wasn't until the end of the second week that the problems at work really began to surface. The students were now becoming more outgoing, but in an aggressive way— more personal questions, more flattery, more flirting. The boys winked, and the girls snickered. Anna was getting absolutely no academic response. All they seemed to want to know about was Anna as a person, not as a teacher. At first, Anna figured that it was all right, because they were speaking English. But over and over again, she let things slide until she became more of a friend to them than an authority figure. This was her final big mistake.

The third week was downright brutal. By this point the students had become almost malicious. Anna had gotten a new class, apparently one that none of the other teachers wanted. Anna had learned by this time to be more firm, but unfortunately the class seemed to have learned about Anna. They seemed to know from the start that she was a lax and easygoing teacher, because right away they began talking and joking around in her class. By the third session, they were speaking in Arabic about her and then turning around and laughing in her face. Not only was this behavior inexcusable, but Anna found it to be incredible. At times she honestly questioned whether some of her students might be mentally retarded. Though most of the ones she taught were in their early twenties, in the classroom they acted more like adolescents. But fortunately, Anna was learning early about the basic mentality of these students and had already made up her mind that she would act upon this knowledge accordingly. Exactly what she would do, she had not yet decided. But she would do something—that she was sure of.

More and more often, as she finished each day, Anna lost no time in leaving the Institute. After her last class, she would walk up to the faculty room, deposit her absentee list, and exit as quickly as possible. She had no desire to see or speak with anybody in that place. The building itself became a symbol of stress and pressure to Anna, something she preferred to avoid to the fullest extent possible. The restaurant, on the contrary, with its sunny terrace and garden, became a place of tranquility and regeneration to her.

Unfortunately, though, the weather was getting cold, as it was now late October. It was a cool day today, so Anna put on her beige raincoat, picked up her purse, and left in a hurry, as usual. When she went into the restaurant this time, she found her new acquaintance eating in the inside dining room. (There was an indoor section to the restaurant as well.) He seemed already to be finishing up his lunch.

Anna stood next to the table, looking very crisp in her tailored raincoat and platform shoes. She was wondering what might be the smartest move to make him follow her out of there. He was probably leaving soon, she thought, so she wouldn't bother to eat. Instead, she would just stand there, hoping he would get the message and get up too.

Once Anna had offered him an inviting smile and handshake, he voluntarily reciprocated. "How's it going?" he said as he greeted her.

"Not so good," she confessed. Then she signaled to him that she didn't want to go into it at that moment. There were other people sitting next to him, and when Anna talked, everybody seemed to listen. She then felt that this was as good a time as any to drop the hint that she wanted to step out with him. "Are you going now?" she asked him, showing neither too much eagerness or apathy.

"Yes, as a matter of fact, I am," he answered, looking down at his empty plate.

Then Anna realized that she had better take the opportunity now before it slipped out of her reach. "I don't think I'm staying either," she said casually. "I'm not hungry anyway."

So they went out together. While they were walking, he asked Anna what was going wrong. This was exactly what she'd had in mind all along. She just wanted somebody to talk to. That's why she pursued him in the way that she did.

"Oh, it's my work," she told him. "It's not going well at all."

"Why not?" he asked.

"If you went into one of my classes, you'd know why not!" she exclaimed. "I just have no discipline at all."

He appeared rather detached, but he still listened. "Don't worry about it," he advised her. "You're not the only teacher who has that problem. They do that with all the new teachers, especially the foreigners."

Eventually, they decided where they wanted to go. They soon found themselves in a small café—one of the more chic and probably more expensive ones. She sat there facing him, with her chin resting in the palm of her hand.

"What's your name, by the way?" she asked.

"Noureddine. How about you?"

"Anna," she answered. "You know, it's funny. I've seen you so many times at the restaurant, but I didn't even know who you were until a couple of days ago. Do you live around here?"

"No, I go to the university nearby, but I get sick and tired of the food at the student restaurant."

Anna didn't want to get into a trite conservation about food again, so she tried to change the subject back to what they had been talking about before. "Oh, really?" she said. "What are you studying over there?"

"Sociology," he said. "I'm in my fourth year there."

They talked for a while—about school, about work, about the weather. Even though Anna had no intention of making a date with him at this time, and he didn't seem to push the idea, either, they seemed to get along well. So when they left each other that day, Anna knew that there would be no personal commitment. Instead, they would probably see each other at the restaurant.

Not only in the classroom was Anna encountering difficulties with her students—it was happening out on the streets as well. All too often Anna would run into students from her classes somewhere in the city. And when they saw Anna, they were just as playful and sarcastic with her as when they were in her classroom. Naturally, Anna was having so much trouble with these students inside the Institute that once she got out of there, they were the last people she wanted to see. But no sooner had she left work to get a bite to eat near the main avenue one afternoon, than she was greeted by a group of about fifteen of her faithful comrades. As far as Anna was concerned, they acted as if they were high on something, laughing and giggling as if they were tripping. As soon as she saw them, Anna literally ran away to be free of them, but they followed her. This time when they approached her, Anna didn't budge. She just stood there calm and cool and trying to make sense out of how her students were communicating with her, but it was no use. The students simply continued ranting and raving just as they did in her classroom, so Anna made up her mind that she was going to lose them, once and for all.

By this time Anna was feeling dizzy. She could see nothing but a bunch of young people laughing and heckling in her face. In a fit of desperation, she ran up to the end of the block and around the corner. When she turned around to find whether any of the students were following her, she saw none of them. Still, she continued racing down the street until she was sure she was rid of them, and finally, it looked as if she was. With all the rushing and commotion, however, Anna had become exhausted and short of breath. She was so drained at this point that she didn't realize she was about ready to faint. Fortunately, though, there was an old Tunisian man nearby who was able to catch her as she fell.

When Anna came to, she found herself in a small but lavishly decorated hut. She was lying on a bed covered with a hand-made quilt, and an old Tunisian woman was sitting over her, fanning her with a trinket made of brightly colored feathers. The woman (probably the wife of the man who found her) was wearing a colorful veil over her head and some heavy jewelry, and had black lines over her face that looked a little like a tattoo but was that horrid make-up women there were often forced to wear. When she saw Anna awaken, the old lady held up a glass of tea to see if she wanted any, but Anna just shook her head. She was still somewhat disoriented and only wanted to leave. Anna slowly got up from the bed, and the woman helped her stand up. On the other side of the room stood the man who had found her. Neither of them spoke French, so Anna thanked them more with gestures than with words for taking her in and caring for her as they had. As the man pulled the tent-like entrance of the hut open, Anna walked out.

On the way back to her apartment, Anna thought about it. The whole incident seemed almost like a dream to her. Had she really been there? Were those two people who found her real—or was she just hallucinating? She had to admit that she had been through so much in such a short amount of time that the stress of it all must have been getting to her. Still, to actually lose consciousness and then to wake up in what seemed to be almost another world was a bit much. Little did Anna know, however, that this would be only the first of many bizarre experiences for her in this unfamiliar country.

The following week at work Anna decided she really had to put her foot down. What the outcome of this would be, she had no idea, but she felt she had to do something. Things started when she went into her first class, where she encountered her students as usual.

"Anna," one of the boys said in English. "How long are you planning to be here?"

"I have a contract for two years."

"Does that mean that you're going to be here for two years?"

"That is the way it's supposed to be," she commented, trying to sound neither indignant nor embarrassed. "What's it to you, anyway?"

"I don't think you should stay here for two years," he said in his somewhat awkward accent. "This is not your place."

This was not her place, Anna thought. She knew where this guy was coming from. What he meant in his distorted form of English was that Anna didn't belong here. So what else is new? Still, she didn't think it was his place to say this. What was his opinion to her anyway?

"Young man," she said coldly. "Perhaps you had better voice your opinion elsewhere. This is my classroom, and it's going to stay that way for a long time."

"So," he said. "It's what I think. That's all."

"I don't care what you think," Anna said, which was nothing less than a lie. "I'm the teacher in this class, and for as long as I'm here, I'll run it as I see fit."

"But I still don't think that this is your place," he said.

That was the last straw. Anna wasn't about to take these insults, especially while the rest of the class was there listening. "Young man," she repeated. "I don't think that this classroom is big enough for the two of us. Maybe you had better leave and not come back until you've changed your attitude."

The boy looked at her oddly, almost as if he didn't understand her version of American slang. Perhaps he was just pretending not to understand, so as to avoid the later consequences. But it was too late. He had pushed Anna too far.

"Why don't you leave right now?" Anna suggested. "It'll be easier for all of us that way."

"I don't want to leave," he said abruptly. "I like this class." Now the boy was finally coming down from his act of arrogance, but it was still too late.

Anna almost laughed out loud. "You just said that you didn't think I had any business being here. After all, this is not my place. Remember?" Her tone was sarcastic but firm and insistent.

"I still don't want to leave," he said. "I want to stay in this class."

"I'm telling you to go!" she ordered the boy. "I want you out of this class right now. Once you've thought about what you said, I'll think about letting you come back."

With that statement, the boy didn't seem to have any more arguments left in him. So he got all his books together, got up from his seat, and left the room. Meanwhile, the rest of the class stared at him as he walked out of the class. He got the message, Anna thought. So without dwelling on the matter any longer, she began her class.

Although she felt she'd had a good result from what had happened in her class that day, Anna could not help but ponder on what the young man had said to her. It was definitely a nasty thing to say to anybody, but wasn't it still true? Anna knew all too well that it was true, but how was she going to hide it from everybody around her? She didn't belong there, and sooner or later, it was going to be apparent to anyone within that Institute. So the only way Anna knew to combat the problem was to stay away from it. This meant to avoid being at her place of employment as much as possible. So this is precisely what she would do.

Since Anna stayed away from the Institute so much, needless to say, she had a lot of spare time on her hands. If it hadn't been for her friend Noureddine, Anna would have been eternally bored. She had already changed her mind about making dates with him, but she still saw him on casual terms. She made simple rendezvous's to go to the movies, to a café, or just for a walk to the Souks. In a way, Anna enjoyed his company, but in another way, she saw him just not to be alone. She felt that most of the men she had met there, she couldn't trust, and that it wasn't worth continuing a relationship with them anyway. Noureddine, however, was somehow different. He had intellect—he had finesse. Not only was he not out for just one thing, he was a serious person about himself and about other people. But there was still something cool and impartial about him— something Anna was aware of and appreciated at the same time. For if he had been too caring, Anna would have known there was a reason behind it.

In contrast with Noureddine's subtle detachment, he was also assertive. He had a way of letting his feelings be known in a discreet fashion. Anna, on the other hand, was strong-willed and had views of her own she demanded to be respected. The two of them ran into their first minor disagreement when they were walking in the Souks one time, just looking around at the various stores. As they were going up the cobblestone alleys, Anna suddenly saw something in one of the shops that really appealed to her.

"Oh, look at this!" she shouted to Noureddine, who was standing right next to her.

Everybody around them turned around and looked at them. This made Noureddine feel uncomfortable. So he quietly approached Anna and told her what he thought of her little act of imprudence. "You know," he said, "When you talk loud like that, you attract unwanted attention."

"Oh, I know," she laughed. "I've been that way for years. It's really terrible."

"Well, don't be that way," he told her, sounding firm and serious.

Then Anna looked him straight in the eye. "What?" she mocked him. "Do you expect me to change overnight?"

"No, I didn't say that. All I meant was that you should try to talk more softly."

"Oh, you're just saying that because you're with me," she said him. "Otherwise, you wouldn't care."

"Of course I care. I just don't want you to talk so loud, that's all." Noureddine managed to remain calm and level-headed throughout the whole discussion.

Anna, meanwhile, was terribly annoyed. What was this guy trying to do, she thought. Take control of me? He hardly knows me. He's got nerve. Anna really did feel provoked. It wasn't so much that she minded being criticized—it was that she just didn't like people trying to move in on her and change her at their discretion. Neither could she stand being treated like a possession. Oh, well, she decided. She would just have to let it slide this time.

Later, however, the situation for both of them seemed to change. That evening they went out to a café. It was an elegant place with a quiet atmosphere. As they were sitting there on the inside terrace, for some reason Anna's hand found itself near Noureddine's on the table. As they were looking down, they both seemed to notice the difference in their skin color. Then he took her hand in his.

"You know," he remarked. "Black really goes well on you." (Anna was wearing a black V-neck blouse.)

Then Anna shrugged. "I guess it's because my skin is so fair," she said. "It's a good contrast."

"I guess so," he agreed. Then he looked at her intently. "You know what I think of when I see you?"

"What?" Anna asked, almost as if she expected to be teased or insulted.

"Your chest is like the sand of the Sahara and your eyes are like the sea." Then he looked at her again, more closely this time. "In the winter I can go swimming in your eyes."

Anna smiled. "Oh, how romantic," she giggled. "How utterly mushy."

It was true, though. They admired each other for completely different reasons. It never crossed Anna's mind, however, that this relationship would lead to anything more serious or lasting. Up until now, it somehow struck her as nothing more than a friendship. But with time Anna would see her interaction with Noureddine develop an entirely new perspective.

One of the reasons Anna was getting so paranoid about her position at work was because she had already had one reprimand from the director. He told her in a nice way that she would have serious problems with the students if she didn't start getting tougher on them damn fast, and that later, such poor discipline might even cause them to go on strike. Anna knew that the director was absolutely right when he talked about her growing behavior problems, but she did not understand what he meant when he said that poor discipline would cause the students to go on strike. Since when do students go on strike? she thought. If anything, she would have assumed that overly strict discipline would cause them to go on strike. Later, though, she would find out exactly what the director was trying to tell her.

Even more disastrous was that every time Anna let things slide, it never failed that somebody was there to see it. During one of Anna's classes, it was well past noon, and it seemed as if all that the students wanted to do was go to lunch. Now they were worse than usual, probably because they were hungry and tired of studying all morning. So instead of waiting until the end of the period, about five minutes before the bell rang, they got up from their seats and stormed out of the classroom, screaming and yelling like a bunch of raving idiots. And who should be standing at the top of the stairs as they went out? None other than the director.

Once again Anna ended up in his office that afternoon. So there she was, sitting on one of his low-seated, upholstered chairs with her arms folded neatly over her knees, listening to him ball her out.

"Miss Daleddo," he shouted. "Within two months time, you have managed to turn this establishment inside out." He was pacing back and forth in front of her.

"I know that, Sir."

"What's more, I told you earlier this year to be more careful," he continued.

"I know that. I never doubted your word."

Then he stopped and turned toward her. "Then why did you let this happen?" he yelled.

"That I don't know, sir. It just happened. That's all."

"That's all," he mocked her. The director then looked at Anna and sighed. He had apparently cooled off by this time. His voice had softened.

Anna just looked down at the floor. She made no effort to defend herself. She said nothing to answer him back. It would have done no good. Besides, everything the director was saying was true. Anna knew she had nothing to fight him with. So, after tolerating his painful reproaches for only a little while longer, she looked up at him and spoke to him in a low and serious voice.

"Can I go now?" she asked him.

Once again the director looked at her and sighed. "Yes, you can," he consented. "But DON'T LET IT HAPPEN AGAIN!" he warned her one last time.

Anna stood up straight and tall, looking at the director face to face. "I'll do what I can," she promised him.

As Anna was walking to the door, the director couldn't help but look her over. His eyes shifted quickly, however, when she turned around. "Good day," she bade him. Then she walked out.

It was now early December. By now Anna felt so lonely and frustrated that she decided to go home for the Christmas holidays, which was only about two weeks away. Despite the fact that the length of her vacation would hardly make the trip worthwhile, Anna felt she was making good enough money to afford it (money she couldn't spend outside of the country anyway). She also figured that there wouldn't be much happening in Tunisia at Christmastide, since it was a Moslem country. So she decided to get her spare cash together, buy a roundtrip ticket to the U.S., and just go there for the holidays.

Before leaving, though, Anna felt she had to say "au revoir" to Noureddine. After all, he was the only friend she had there in Tunis. Though she had never given her address to Noureddine, she had already been to his place several times. None of the times she had been there, however, had she stayed for very long. She didn't really want to. For one thing, she didn't like his room—it was dirty and poorly furnished. For another, she was afraid of his trying anything. But despite her fears, he never did.

So one afternoon, not long before she was planning to leave, Anna went over to see Noureddine at his home. He lived in one of the secluded neighborhoods in the Medina. Since she had no written address, and this was the first time she had ever gone there by herself, Anna had a devil of a time finding the place. She did not even know the name of the street. All she remembered was that when she went there with Noureddine, they had both taken a shortcut through a small alley that led directly to his home. So once she had gone through this direct route, Anna recognized the place immediately, because it had no roof on the inside—just an open courtyard. The building itself stood out to Anna. She knew also that his room was on the second level. So she quickly climbed the stairs, went to his door, and knocked on it loudly.

Since it was the middle of the day, she would be lucky to find him there. Nevertheless, right away somebody answered from inside. "Who is it?" he called.

"Anna," she replied. She felt very relieved to know that he was in.

"Oh!" Noureddine hurried to the door and opened it. "How are you doing?" he grinned. He acted happy to see her.

"OK, I guess."

When she went in, Anna could not hide a slight frown. Noureddine's room consisted of four dirty walls, an unmade bed, and a desk and chair. There were books and papers galore, even on the floor. The room even smelled musty. Anna often asked herself how he could live in a place like that.

"Do sit down," he said politely. Noureddine had to clear away some folders and papers before Anna could have a seat on the bed. Apparently, he had been studying before she came.

Careful not to give any inviting signs, Anna took her coat off and sat primly on the bed. "The reason I came is to say 'goodbye,'" she told him.

"Oh, really?" he said as he sat down next to her.

"Yes, I'm leaving for the U.S. on Saturday," she explained. "But I'll be coming back after Christmas vacation."

"Oh, I see." He looked relieved to know that she wasn't leaving for good. "What made you decide to go all the way home just for the holidays?"

"Oh, you know all the problems that I've been having at work," she reminded him. "Now they've only gotten worse, and I thought that getting away from the whole situation might do me some good."

"I suppose so," he surmised. "But isn't it expensive?"

"Yes, very," she said, nodding her head. "But there's a certain amount of money that I have to spend in the country anyway. It's part of my contract."

"Oh, I see," he said again. "You know, I've always wanted to go to the United States, at least to visit."

"Oh," Anna laughed. "I've heard that 'song and dance' so many times. All my friends that I meet abroad say the same thing. But to date not one of them has ever come to the U.S."

"No, I'm serious," he insisted. "I'm going to do it some day."

"Yeah, sure," Anna humored him. "Maybe you will do it someday."

"You know, I'm going to miss seeing you at the restaurant these next couple of weeks." He touched her shoulder, but before he even had the chance to put his arm around her, Anna quickly stood up and scurried over to the chair on the other side of the room.

"Come back over here," Noureddine said, pointing to the empty space beside him on the bed.

"No," Anna said with a smile. "I'm fine over here."

"Come over here where you were before," he implored her. "I'm not going to do anything."

Finally, Anna decided to take his word for it. She went over and sat next to him again and stayed there this time. Noureddine also kept his promise. He did not try to touch her again. They talked for a while, mostly about the United States. Would he ever really go there? Anna wondered. She doubted it. In her own mind, though, she wanted to believe that he really would make the trip someday. Anna had to admit that she liked Noureddine very much, but she did not love him—or at least that is what she thought at the time. At any rate, when they bade each other "au revoir" that day, Anna was sure she would be seeing Noureddine again.

Friday evening, Anna packed her bags to leave early Saturday morning. It wasn't a complicated procedure, as she was leaving most of her things there in the apartment for when she came back. Once again, Anna sat on her bed and stared into the huge antique mirror facing her. Then she looked at the small tapestry suitcase she was taking with her. Despite her relatively trivial reasons for going home, Anna was glad she doing it. She felt happy about seeing her parents and brother again, even though it had only been a few months since the last time they had all been together. She was anxious to find out how they were, as well as to tell them about her own experiences. The problem was that she was not aware of the turmoil going on within her own family at this very moment. For little did Anna know that going home at this time would be her biggest mistake yet.

Chapter 5

Anna arrived at the Baltimore-Washington Airport late Saturday night. As she had specified the flight number and arrival time on a telegram she had sent out to her parents before she left Tunis, Anna expected to find at least one person there waiting for her. However, after she went through customs and claimed her baggage, Anna found no one she recognized within the terminal. She waited at least a half hour, not budging from the baggage claim for fear that she might miss whoever was coming to the airport to pick her up.

Finally, Anna saw her mother, Louise, coming through the terminal. She was walking slowly along the carpeted runway. When she saw her daughter waiting for her, instead of looking happy to see her again, Louise had a rather distressed look on her face. Anna greeted her mother with a kiss, but Louise still seemed unresponsive. Anna could tell that there was something wrong.

"Why were you so late?" she inquired. "Car trouble?"

"No, not exactly." Even Louise's voice was subdued.

A feeling of uneasiness came over Anna as she noticed her mother's troubled state of mind, so she felt it was better just to get the whole problem out in the open. "Hey, what's the matter?" she asked bluntly. "What's going on?"

Louise hesitated a bit, wringing her hands nervously as she stared down at the floor. "Let's go have some coffee somewhere, and I'll tell you what's the matter," she promised. "There's no point in hiding it now."

"OK," Anna nodded solemnly. "Let's go then." So together they went to a coffee shop inside the terminal.

Louise was just below medium height, but a slim woman who looked much younger than her fifty years. She was fair, like Anna, but with a rosy complexion that gave her a lot of natural color. Even her short, styled hair had a reddish tinge to it. Most of the time she preferred to wear sweaters and blue jeans—one reason for her youthful appearance. Yet in some ways, she had more of a flair in her dressing than Anna did. More often than not, she dolled herself up tastefully with makeup and jewelry.

Once the two of them had found a shop that suited them, they settled at a table and were served some coffee almost immediately. "So what's the problem?" Anna asked again.

"It's Paul," Louise finally confessed. "I don't know what's the matter with him."

"Paul?" Anna repeated. "Is he sick?"

"No, not exactly."

"So what's the matter then?"

"He seems to be having emotional problems," Louise admitted. "Friday night he came home all uptight. He hasn't calmed down since."

Then Anna slanted her eyebrows. "All uptight?" she repeated. "What does that mean?"

"He's just very nervous," Louise said. "I really couldn't tell you anything more."

"When did all this come about?" Anna inquired.

"Oh, I don't know," Anna's mother sighed. "It's probably been building up for a long time. Last week Addie called to tell us that she thought Paul was unhappy down there. She said that she just had to do something about it."

Anna stared at her mother. Then it dawned on Louise that she wasn't paying enough attention to her daughter.

"I'm sorry, Annie," she apologized. "I'm so caught up in Paul's problems that I've completely forgotten to ask about you. What made you want to come home for the holidays, anyway?"

This made Anna feel very uneasy. She couldn't tell her mother the truth—not now, anyway. She realized that Louise would really be upset if she knew that her daughter was also unhappy. "I just wanted to come home," she said in a flustered voice. "I just wanted to see you all."

"Are you sure there isn't more to it than that?" Louise asked. "It seems rather strange that you would come all this way for two weeks just to see us."

"Of course, I'm sure," Anna insisted. "I just wanted to see you, that's all."

Louise's expression was still withdrawn. "I honestly wonder if it would have been better for you not to come at all, since this is such a depressing situation," she remarked. "But I guess it's too late to think about that now."

"Yeah, I guess so," Anna agreed. Then abruptly, she changed the subject. "But how about if we go home now? I'm not looking forward to facing Paul in his present condition, but I know I'll have to do it sooner or later. So we might as well make it now."

"All right," Louise agreed. "Let's go."

As they were driving home, Anna began to feel more and more tense. The ride seemed to take forever. As it was rather late, the highway was dark and lonely, which made her feel that much more dejected. It almost seemed as if they were taking some unknown route that led to no destination.

At last they arrived at the house. Louise pulled into the driveway and parked the car. She helped Anna with her suitcase, taking it out of the car for her and setting it outside on the pavement. Although it was now almost midnight, the house was still lighted up. Before she had time to think about what was to come, Anna walked quickly to the back door, her mother following with the suitcase. She pulled open the screen door and went in. Her father was out for the evening, so nobody was in the house but Paul. When he heard Anna come in, he walked into the kitchen.

At first, Anna saw no noticeable change in her brother. He looked as trim and well groomed as ever. When she approached him, however, she saw the difference in his face, noticing especially a change in his eyes. They stared at her senselessly, almost frightfully. It was as if he were looking through Anna and not at her. He didn't seem at all phased by her arrival, considering especially that she had come such a long way.

"How are you doing?" Anna said.

"OK, I guess." There was still not much reaction on Paul's part to his sister's presence.

"Paul," Anna said in a straightforward manner. "What seems to be the problem? What's been going on with you?"

Paul seemed pleased that Anna was willing to talk about him rather than herself. "I think I'm suffering from severe feelings of guilt," he said, sounding almost like a psychiatrist.

"Feelings of guilt?" Anna questioned. "Guilt about what?"

"Oh, I'm thinking about what happened at Steamers during the whole time I was there," he explained. "I was fired from that job, you know."

"Fired?" Anna didn't know that Paul had been dismissed from his previous position, so now she really was confused.

"Actually, I was 'asked to quit,' " he said, "but that's pretty much the same thing."

Anna just stood there, trying to make some sense of what Paul was telling her. She was so overwrought and exhausted from her trip and now from this sudden news that she wasn't thinking straight. "Hold on for a second, Paul," she said, trying to contain herself. "Let me get myself together here, and then we'll sit down and talk about it."

Anna put her suitcase in her room and then slipped into something more comfortable. When she went back into the kitchen, she saw that Paul was still there, looking as distraught as ever. Without saying anything to him, Anna made them both some tea, poured it into a pot, and set it on the kitchen table.

Sitting at the table, Paul found himself so close to Anna that he suddenly, yet tenderly, took her hand in his. This shocked Anna, as Paul had never done this before in his life. "Annie," he said, leaning close to her. "I don't mind telling you, I can't wait to get out of this thing."

This thing, Anna thought. What thing? It almost sounded to her as if Paul were talking from inside a cage or a cell or if he were trapped inside some small, confined dwelling. Now Anna was worried about her brother. Now she could see that Paul was quite out of touch with the real world.

"Paul, I don't understand what's going on," she said, clutching his hand tightly. "Things seemed to be going so well for you a couple of months ago. What's the matter now?"

"Everything's the matter," he said. "Just everything." Paul shook his head and stared down at the table.

Anna slowly slid her hand out of her brother's. What could she do to help him, when she realized she wasn't even communicating with him? She knew that he was expressing only words, not ideas or feelings, and that he wasn't making any sense at all.

"Paul," she continued. "I don't know if this will make you feel any better, but I came home for the exact same reason. My job is going down the tubes. I don't even know how long I'm going to last there."

Paul did not respond to this last statement. It seemed almost as if he didn't see or hear anything going on around him. Instead, he just took the pot and poured himself a cup of tea. When they both had finished, they got up and went to their rooms. Before she went to bed, Anna thought about it. It doesn't make sense, she said to herself. It all just doesn't make sense. Why would Paul suddenly freak out like this, when he had so much going for him before? Little did Anna know that she had not seen the half of it. If she thought Paul was freaking out now, all she had to do was wait and see what would happen as time went on.

The next day Paul was in a considerably worse state. Also in the house was Robert, Anna and Paul's father. Seeing him for the first time since he had been home, Anna noted that he seemed preoccupied with his son's condition. Anna greeted her father cordially, but before she had time to talk to him, Paul came in with his own problems. Not only was Paul perpetually involved with himself, he also seemed to have physical symptoms he could not control. He couldn't stop walking around, often stretching his arms and legs in an exaggerated fashion, and he held onto his parents like an infant or small child.

When Anna saw her brother in one of these states, she stared at him out of the corner of her eye. At times like these, she became increasingly exasperated. When she found that Paul was having a fit like this, she became alarmed and had to go to her room and lock the door. She was so disturbed by these ugly scenes that she could no longer bear to witness them. Anna felt that she didn't know her brother anymore. Somehow, she knew she never would again.

Since Anna was perplexed by this situation, the natural thing to do was to ask her parents about it. The one who seemed to know the most about what was going on was Louise, because she had spent a lot of time with Paul when he was still living at home. So the next morning, Anna sat down in the kitchen with her mother and, while she was having a cup of coffee, started to inquire as to what caused Paul to end up in the state he was now in.

"There seem to be some things about Paul's job situation that I did not know," Anna remarked.

"That is an understatement," Louise agreed. "As a matter of fact, there are many things I did not know about until recently."

"Oh, really?" Anna responded. "Like what?"

"Well, it was obvious that Paul was not particularly happy, even when he was working at Steamers. He said he was not making any sales there and that all he ever seemed to do was hang out with a coworker named Danny."

"Oh. Danny," Anna recalled. "Somehow, I remember Paul talking about him."

"Anyway, it turned out that this Danny was an unscrupulous bastard who said something bad about Paul to their boss, and then the boss got mad and fired them both."

Anna was still a bit confused. "But if Paul landed a better job anyway, what does it matter? I mean, all that happened at Steamers is water under the bridge."

"Well," Louise went on. "You know that Paul at least had friends in this area when he was working at Steamers, but now I'm under the impression that he was lonely down in Greensboro. Paul blamed Danny for his having lost all that when he was fired from Steamers."

"But how is his new job down in Greensboro going?" Anna asked. "Isn't that the most important thing right now?"

"That's another problem," Louise stated. "I suspect that Paul isn't doing any better at this new job than he was at his old one. In fact, I have a good hunch that Paul was deathly afraid of getting fired again. It almost seems as if he was getting completely paranoid."

"Well I hope things are at least working out for him living with Aunt Addie," Anna commented.

"That's still another problem," Louise added. "Paul says that living with somebody so elderly and eccentric is turning out to be extremely difficult."

Hearing all this, Anna sat back in her chair. "I hate to say 'I told you so,' but I was very skeptical about the whole idea of Paul moving down to North Carolina. There was something about it that seemed too good to be true."

"It looks as if you were right," Louise nodded. "At times I get the same feeling."

Not having much more to say, and also having finished her coffee, Anna got up from the table and put her cup and saucer in the sink. Before she left the kitchen, however, she turned to her mother one more time. "I hope Paul can straighten things out very soon," she said. "Because if he can't, I have a feeling he may not be able to straighten them out at all."

One evening the following week as Anna was getting ready to go out, she overheard Robert, Louise, and their son talking about Paul's previous job. Paul was telling about all of his horrible experiences at Steamers—how he felt so belittled and disgraced there, how other people there pushed him out, how he was forced to find another job, and more. Along with his talking, Paul seemed to be doing quite a bit of drinking. Although not exactly drunk, he appeared to be under the influence. He was, in fact, just enough under the influence to be able to alter his mood at will. That was exactly what he did that evening.

Not long after they started this crucial discussion, Paul abruptly announced a complete change in his outlook on life. "Hey," he said, looking up at his parents. "I've recovered. I've absolutely recovered. I realize that I have a better job than they do now. I'm the one who's ahead."

"Oh, you're high now," Robert warned him. "Things wouldn't change that fast for you."

"Oh no, this is for real," Paul insisted. "You should see my office at Mackenfield. It's really great. At Steamers I had to share one with three other guys. Now I know that I'm the one who's ahead. I'm completely cured."

Paul was soon up and about, walking around constantly. He was in such a good mood that he decided to go out and see some of the old gang that he used to hang out with. This concerned his parents even more, as they knew that his good mood wouldn't last forever and that when he did get out of it, he would probably feel lower than he had before. They tried several times to caution him that this frame of mind would not last long, but it did no good. Paul was determined to go out and get it all together again. Anna, meanwhile, was going out regardless of what Paul decided to do.

That night when Anna came back from her date, it was well past midnight. Her parents and brother were already sleeping, or so she thought. The hallway and bedrooms were all dark. As her room was right next to Paul's, Anna was careful not to make much noise when she got ready for bed. However, the minute he heard that she was there, Paul called to Anna from inside his room.

"Annie, come here."

Anna went to his room and opened the door. "What is it, Paul?" she asked.

"Turn on the light," he demanded. Anna reached for the switch on the wall. Paul was lying on his bed, stiff on his back, with just a sheet covering his body.

"Tonight I saw somebody who knows some of my old friends from Steamers," he told her. "They all know what happened there. They all know it, Annie. They know that I'm crazy."

Anna did not know how to respond. The more she heard of this kind of talk, the less she knew about how to deal with it. Again, she felt so ill at ease with this scene that she literally did not want to see what was going on. So in an instant, she flicked off the light. Nevertheless, she approached his bed and proceeded to offer him the most practical advice she could think to give somebody like that.

"Paul," she said. "This is going to sound kind of corny, but have you ever thought of getting professional help?" Anna felt silly suggesting such a thing, but it didn't matter, because as usual, Paul wasn't listening.

"No, Annie," he said. "It's too late. I'm crazy. That's all there is to it."

Anna didn't know what else to say or do, so she gave him what she considered to be the second most practical piece of advice to somebody in Paul's condition. "Why don't you go to sleep, Paul?" she said. "I'm sure you'll feel better in the morning."

Slowly and quietly, Anna walked out of Paul's room, closed the door, and tiptoed back to her own room, where she turned off the light and climbed into bed. As much as she had tried to be reassuring to Paul as well as to herself, Anna could not help but feel distraught. Neither could she help but ponder over what was happening day and night. What was it in Paul that was making him react in such a frightfully dramatic fashion? What was it about these jobs that could have been all that important? Anna had no idea as to what the answers to these questions really were. Once again, what she did not realize at this time was that when she finally did learn the truth about her brother, it would be far too late for everybody involved.

Only a couple of hours had passed before Anna was awakened by the sudden sound of footsteps. It was a light tapping noise, as if someone were walking around barefoot. Anna got up, put on her robe, and went down the hall to find out what it was. In the living room Anna saw that it was Paul who had gotten up, and that now he was sitting on the sofa in the dark. He appeared to be staring out of the picture window, with the moonlight shining on him.

"Paul," she said. "What are you doing up at this hour?"

Paul turned his head slowly, not looking the least bit affected by Anna's presence. Instead, he reacted to her in a sober fashion, answering her in a solemn voice. "Why shouldn't I be up at this hour? I can't sleep."

As Anna approached Paul, she noticed that he was shaking like a leaf. When she got even closer, she saw that he was half nude, wearing only a pajama bottom. "Paul," she gasped. "You'll catch pneumonia like that."

In a flash, Anna took off her woolen robe and put it around her brother's shoulders. Paul listlessly took his arms and pulled the robe up around his chest. Soon the shivering subsided, and Paul seemed more sedate, but no more responsive.

"Paul," Anna said, sitting down beside him. "Why don't you go back to bed? Staying up like this isn't going to do you any good."

Paul was still looking out the picture window. "Going back to bed isn't going to do me any good either," he commented. "Because in the morning I'll just have to wake up again."

Anna got the gist of what her brother was saying. Staying awake wasn't the answer—and going to sleep wasn't either. If he went to sleep, he would have to wake up sooner or later. In a way, Anna knew her brother was right. So rather than argue with him, she just sat there next to him on the sofa and stared at the shadows the moon was making as it shined in through the picture window.

"Annie," Paul said, finally looking at her. "You know what I wish?"

"What do you wish?"

"I wish I could go into an eternal sleep—one where I could rest forever."

"What do you mean by that?" Anna challenged him, acting almost as if she were afraid of the answer.

"You know what I mean," Paul said insistently. "I wish I could go into a sleep where I wouldn't have to wake up at all. That way my problems would be over, once and for all."

Anna didn't want to hear any more. She knew what Paul was getting at, and the more she heard of this conversation, the more distressed she became. So before he could blurt out another word regarding his own fate, she felt that she had to try to convince him to go back to bed.

"How about if we both try to get some sleep?" Anna suggested, now trying to sound more assertive than she did the time before.

Paul still seemed indifferent to the idea, but finally nodded his head. "All right," he said, getting up from the sofa. "I'll try to get some sleep, for what it's worth."

Then Anna got up, too. Since Paul was still shivering, even with her robe around him, she did not ask for it back. Instead, she followed him down the hall until she got to her bedroom door. They both went into their own rooms, closed the doors, and went back to bed.

The next morning Anna woke up around eleven o'clock. She got up and went into the kitchen. There she found her mother sitting alone at the table, drinking some coffee. Anna could tell by Louise's expression that something was on her mind. As always, Anna chose to get right to the point.

"Hi, Mom," she said casually. "You have something you want to tell me?"

Louise was already acting self-conscious, which made Anna even more certain that her mother had something to say to her. The only question she had now was exactly what it was. Anna would find out soon enough.

"Annie," she said, looking down at her coffee. "Your father and I have been talking about you."

"About me?" Anna acted surprised that they weren't spending all their time discussing Paul's problems for a change. "What in the world would you have to say about me?"

Louise hesitated for a moment but then came right out with it. "We were talking about you and the job you have over in Tunisia."

"So? What about it?"

"Why don't you sit down?" Louise suggested. "It's better if we talk about this together."

Anna pulled out a chair and sat down. "So what was this all-important conversation about?" she asked anxiously.

"Annie," Louise said again. "Your father and I don't think you should go back to that job at all. We think you should stay home, since you're back here anyway."

Anna placed both her hands firmly on the table and leaned toward her mother, looking her straight in the eye. "What?" she exclaimed. "Are you out of your mind?"

"I know it sounds like a crazy idea," Louise admitted. "But we feel that you should at least give it some thought."

"Oh," Anna groaned. "That idea is more than just crazy. It's completely out of the question."

"Out of the question?" Louise echoed. "You don't have to go back there. Nobody's forcing you."

"But who is forcing me to stay here?" Anna argued. "Hasn't it crossed your mind that I would want to go back?"

"Of course it has," Louise replied. "But have you ever considered the possible consequences of going back there?"

"Consequences. What consequences?"

"You know, you might encounter some problems that you won't be able to deal with."

"What makes you want to come to all these conclusions? Whatever gave you these ideas?"

"I-I just thought that it might not be worth it for you to go back to your job," Louise said. "Besides, I got the impression that you didn't like it there anyway."

"Yes," Anna granted. "But there's more to your presumptions than just the fact that I don't like it there. This has something to do with what's happening to Paul, doesn't it?"

Louise knew that what her daughter was saying was true. "All right," she confessed, "it does. I'm afraid that if you go back to that job, the same thing will happen to you as has happened to Paul."

Not only was Anna insulted by what Louise was saying, she was also downright angry. What gave her mother the right to make such a prediction, especially when it was based on what was going on with somebody else? Anna was not the same person as Paul, and she would certainly not tolerate being treated accordingly.

"I'm sorry, Mother," she told her. "But I can't let an assumption concerning Paul guide my own destiny. I must do what I must do, and that is it. If that doesn't make you happy, then you're the one who has to deal with it."

Louise gave a reluctant sigh, but finally gave in to her daughter's wishes. "All right," she said. "Have it your way, but don't say I didn't warn you."

"I won't," Anna promised. "Whatever I do in my life, I'll be responsible for my own actions. You can be sure of that."

Unlike Anna, Louise couldn't be sure of anything. She simply could not help but think that the same thing that had happened to Paul would repeat itself for Anna. Still, she had no choice but to accept her daughter's decision to return to her job. Louise got up from the table and went to her room, leaving Anna alone in the kitchen.

The ugly scenes with Paul were not over, at least not for as long as Anna was there. One evening Anna and her mother were sitting in the den, watching the late news on television. They were both stretched out on a large, three-sided sofa that could easily serve as a bed. Other than the glow of the television, there was no other light in the room. Louise and Anna had their backs propped up against the huge cushions on the sofa, and they were both drinking wine.

At last the evening news was over, and the late movie came on. The two of them felt relaxed and intended to stay that way. Though neither of them were aware of it, Paul appeared in the doorway of the den. He just stood there, not saying or doing anything to attract their attention. When they finally did notice that he was there, they were a bit startled. When he approached them, Anna saw that Paul was again less than appropriately dressed, wearing just a pajama bottom and shivering from head to toe. As always, the closer he came to her, the more uncomfortable she felt.

"Mom," he said, now standing in front of Louise. "I'm afraid of dying. I really am." Then he took a few steps closer to her. "I don't want to die, but I'm afraid I might. I really do." Paul finally went over to the sofa and sat next to his mother. "Hold me, Mom," he begged, now leaning his body against hers. "You can save me from dying. I know you can."

Louise took Paul in her arms, so that his head was resting on her chest. After only a few seconds of softly stroking and caressing her son's body, Louise suddenly broke down and began to weep, crying so quietly that even Anna could not hear her.

"Paul," Louise said, trying to hide her tears. "Why don't you go back to bed and try to get some sleep? You just need some rest, that's all."

Paul had heard this advice so many times before and it did him so little good to heed it, but this time he lifted his head and looked at Louise. "All right," he said calmly. "I'll go back to bed and try to get some sleep." Without so much as looking at Anna, Paul got up from the sofa and walked out of the room.

Anna had observed them the whole time that Paul was in the room. Honestly, she thought to herself. Couldn't anybody get a minute's peace in this house? What Paul was putting his parents through was unimaginable. They didn't deserve that. Really, they didn't.

Anna sighed as she got up from the sofa, picking her empty wine glass from off the table. Louise was sitting still, looking down at her own glass. Anna turned and looked at her mother.

"Mom," she said, "I don't know what to say or do to help. I suppose that's why I'm going back to Tunisia. If I thought that staying home would do any good, I would do it. I know it won't, so I have to go back."

The Sunday before she was to go back to work, Anna went out to dinner with her parents. Paul did not attend. He said he didn't feel up to coming along. He wouldn't have enjoyed himself anyway.

Anna had already spent the entire Christmas and New Year holidays with her family, and now it was almost over. It hadn't really seemed like a holiday at all. During this vacation there wasn't that feeling of celebration in the household that normally would have been present at this time of year. Throughout the whole visit, Anna had less of a chance to talk with her father than she'd had with her mother. Robert was concerned about his son and not having much time to spend with his daughter. But finally, Anna would have a chance to interact with her father.

Robert was a small, rather distinguished looking man, with dark hair gray at the temples and very blue eyes. He was also quite fair, considering that he was of Italian descent. He spoke like the educated person he was, often using words that even his family did not understand. In personality, Anna was very much like her father. Like Robert, she had a keen, perceptive mind and was a profound thinker. She had also inherited two outstanding personality traits from him: absent-mindedness and obliviousness. Both of them had the amazing ability to dismiss themselves from their present company and its demands any time they wanted to. They were rarely self conscious and didn't particularly care about what others thought of them. They were completely and totally individualistic, and they were both a hundred percent intellectual.

The whole time they were eating their meal at the restaurant, both Robert and Louise acted preoccupied, as if they had something weighing on their minds. It was a cinch for Anna to figure out what it was. But sooner or later they both would come out with it anyway.

"Annie," Robert said solemnly. "Are you sure you want to go back to that job?"

"Yes, I'm sure," she replied bluntly.

"I don't mind telling you, I was against this idea from the start, and I still am," Robert said.

"I know. But like I said, I must do what I must do. Believe it or not, I'm just as concerned about Paul as you are, but I feel that staying home and obsessing over Paul's problems would do him more harm than good. If anything, I may be able to set an example for him by returning to Tunisia."

"Annie," Louise cut in. "I don't know if you believe this or not, but we're just as concerned about your welfare as we are about Paul's. We don't care about your setting an example for anybody. We just think that you might not profit from going back there."

"So?" Anna retorted. "How am I going to profit from staying here? There's nothing for me here anyway."

Then both of her parents finally gave in. "Do what you want," Robert conceded. "I only hope that you won't regret your decision."

"Annie," Louise said once more. "Just remember one thing. If you feel that you can't take it, leave the job. Don't wait until it's too late."

Too late? Anna thought. In a sense, wasn't it already too late? For Paul, it was too late in that he had waited too long before he got help. For Anna, it was too late in that she had already gotten involved with this job. Anna felt trapped. She wanted as desperately to help her brother as she wanted to help herself. But she meant every word that she had said to her parents. She had to go back to prove her degree of perseverance to her parents, to Paul, and most of all, to herself. Now Anna felt as ready as she ever would be to return to her job.

So two days later, Anna flew back to Tunis.

Chapter 6

When Anna returned to Tunis, it was already early January. The weather was cold, and the sky was gray. Now it was officially winter in Tunisia. Outside, it was so bleak, in fact, that Anna wondered what would have been worse: staying home with her family—or living here now. At any rate, she was back at her job, whether she liked it or not.

Once she had recuperated from her trip back, one of the first things Anna wanted to do was to see Noureddine again. Though their relationship was almost platonic, Anna had to admit that she really enjoyed being with him. It was nice to know that she had at least one friend where she was living right now. Anna wondered if it would appear too forward of her to go to his room to see him again. It crossed her mind that he might reject her, especially after what had happened the last time she was there. Nevertheless, she really had nothing to lose by stopping by to pay him a visit, so she made up her mind that she would do it.

A few days after she had returned to Tunis, Anna went to where Noureddine lived. She got as far as the doorstep without any problem. At that moment, though, she hesitated and felt uneasy. He's going to give me the brush-off, she told herself. She stood in front of the door for a few seconds before she finally got up the courage to knock on it.

Almost immediately, a familiar voice answered. "Yes? Who is it?"

"It's Anna," she replied.

Then she heard somebody walk to the door and open it. There stood Noureddine, looking as if he had been in his usual turmoil of studying. As always, he looked delighted to see her. "How are you doing?" he greeted her, almost putting his arm around her as if to invite her in.

"Fine," she said, as she walked into his room.

As usual, Noureddine's room was a total mess, with books and papers all over the floor. "I didn't expect you to be back here so soon," he said. "How was your trip to the U.S.?"

"Oh, it was terrible. It was the biggest mistake I ever made in my life."

"Oh?" Noureddine responded. "How's that?" He sat on a chair facing Anna, who had taken off her coat and was sitting on his bed.

"It's my brother. He seems to be having severe emotional problems."

"Emotional problems?" Noureddine repeated. "What do you mean by that?"

"It's a long story," Anna sighed. "Right now, suffice it to say that his job isn't going well, and he seems to be taking it too seriously." Then she turned and looked at Noureddine. "But let's talk about you for a change. How's everything going these days?"

"OK, I guess," he replied. "But you know, I really missed you these last couple of weeks."

"Oh, I bet," Anna joked. "You were probably too busy burying yourself in your books to worry about me."

"What?" Noureddine retorted. "You think the only thing I do is study? I have the normal impulses of a man, you know."

Anna didn't know how to react. She knew darn well what he meant by the comment, but she didn't know whether to feel attracted or repelled by it. She knew only that she wasn't ready to feel either way toward Noureddine.

"I never doubt your word," Anna responded. "But I honestly question how much you were thinking about me over the holidays."

"Of course I was thinking about you over the holidays," Noureddine said, smiling. "Who else would I be thinking about?"

Without waiting for a response from her, Noureddine got up from his seat, went over to the bed, and sat next to Anna. This time, she did not run away. Instead, she leaned her body close to his as he circled his arm around her. They just sat there for a while, not saying anything at all. Even so, the intimacy and trust seemed to agree with both of them for a change.

Soon Anna figured that it was as good a time as any to leave. "Hey," she said, turning and looking at Noureddine. "I've got to go now."

"As you wish," Noureddine said. "But it's getting kind of late, so let me walk you at least part of the way home."

"OK," Anna agreed. So as soon as they got their things together, the two of them left the room, with Noureddine locking the door securely behind him.

While he was walking her home, he said, "After I have earned my degree here in Tunis, I'm thinking of going to the United States to live."

"Hmmm," Anna said as she shrugged. "How long have you been planning to do this?" For ten minutes? she thought.

"Oh, for quite a while," Noureddine replied. "It's only a question of finding the means to do it."

Anna did not respond to what Noureddine was saying to her, as she understood exactly where he was coming from. Really, she thought. Talk about jumping the gun!

When they got to the main avenue, Anna politely thanked Noureddine for accompanying her that far and bade him "good night." When she got home, however, Anna thought about what had happened a while ago. Is it possible? she asked herself. It all seemed to have come about so suddenly. Yet it hadn't. She had known this young man for so long without feeling anything toward him. She didn't think that much about him. She didn't even like him to touch her. Now all at once, these sentiments seemed to be changing.

Anna was afraid. She was afraid of getting too attached to any one person. She was afraid of the rapport that would follow. She was afraid of its later consequences. Was it true? she questioned. Was this really love, or was it just a silly whim that would pass her by later on? Oh well, she thought. She would find the answers to these questions as time went on, when everything would become clearer.

About a week passed. Meanwhile, things had not improved a great deal with Anna's job. A bigger problem for her was that she couldn't stop thinking about herself in relationship to Paul. The more she worked, the more she understood her brother's problems—problems she never thought existed until now. An even bigger fear for Anna was that she might react to them in the same way Paul had. As much as she hated to admit it, Anna knew, deep down inside, that her parents might have been right. She realized that, whether she was like Paul or not, there was always the pending possibility that the same thing might happen to her as had already happened to him.

By this time, Anna had already received a letter from her parents saying that Paul was OK—that he was neither good nor bad. Anna was not particularly impressed by what she was being told. It all sounded rather ambiguous to her. It really didn't matter, anyway. She had a fairly good hunch that if and when something did happen, her parents would tell her immediately. Unfortunately for Anna, this assumption would turn out to be all too true.

One morning when Anna stopped by Noureddine's place, she found that he wasn't there. As she hadn't seen him in over a week, she decided to leave him a note to see her that afternoon. After that, she went to work.

As soon as Anna arrived at the Institute that day, she was approached by one of the Tunisian teachers from the English department. "Are you Miss Daleddo?" she asked in her Oxford accent.

"I certainly am," Anna smiled.

"There was a phone call for you earlier this morning. The secretary told them that you would be in later on."

Anna's pleasant expression faded. "Who was it from?"

"I don't know," the woman responded. "All I know is that it was an international call—from the U.S., probably."

"Yeah, probably." Then Anna turned and looked at the woman. "Thank you for telling me this," she said. "I'll be waiting for them to call me again."

"Of course," she said. Then the woman walked away.

Anna refused even to guess as to what the telephone call was about. Actually, she didn't even know for certain who it was from. From her parents, probably. But what about? Paul or herself? Anna shrugged. There she was, guessing when she had promised herself that she wouldn't. Oh, well. Anna realized that she would just have to wait until she heard from them again to find out what the call was about. So that morning Anna started working quite normally, trying as much as possible to forget about what she had just been told.

When she finished her work that day, Anna was in more of a hurry than usual to leave the Institute. She was so nervous about what had happened earlier that morning that she wanted desperately to avoid it this time. Just as she was headed down the stairs, however, the director's secretary called her over.

"Miss Daleddo," she said, holding the telephone in her hand. "This is for you."

Anna walked over to the secretary's desk. She took the phone from her and put it to her ear. Then she reluctantly began to talk. "Hello?...Oh, hi!...I'm fine, but why are call-ing?...Paul? What about him?...What kind of hospital?...He had a nervous breakdown?...Oh, God!"

Without saying another word on the telephone, Anna hung up the phone abruptly. As quickly as possible, she got her things together and left the Institute. When she got to her apartment, no one was there. She went into her room and threw her coat and other things on the bed. Not knowing what else to do, Anna paced for a while. Soon enough, though, somebody rang at the door downstairs. When Anna opened her bedroom window and looked down to the street, she saw Noureddine standing on the sidewalk. Never before in her life had she been so glad to see him.

"Oh, Noureddine!" she called to him. She spoke in such a distressed voice that he knew right away that some-thing was wrong.

"Anna, are you all right?" he asked, looking up at her.

"I don't know." Her voice was quivering.

"Come down and let me in," he said. "Then you can tell me what's going on."

Before he knew it, Noureddine found himself in Anna's bedroom for the first time. So there he was, sitting on a desk chair, facing Anna as she sat on the edge of the bed. Now he was beginning to understand why Anna was so upset.

"It's my brother," she explained. "It's finally hap-pened."

"What finally happened?"

"He had a nervous breakdown," she groaned. "Now he's locked up in some hospital ward."

"How did you find this out?"

"My parents gave me a call at the Institute. I guess they didn't want to tell me something like that in a letter."

"I can understand that," Noureddine agreed. "But why did this happen to your brother?"

93

"Oh, who knows?" Anna speculated. "In a way I feel like the breakdown was happening while I was still at home. Now it's just a question of his being hospitalized. But why? Nobody knows the answer to that."

At that moment, Noureddine went over and sat next to her on the bed. "Don't take it so hard," he advised. "After all, you've got your own life to live. We all do."

"Yeah," Anna replied. "I guess you're right on that score."

Then Noureddine looked at her. "Are you feeling better, Anna?"

"Call me Annie," she told him. "Everybody who knows me well does."

"OK," he agreed. "Are you feeling better, Annie?"

"Yes," she nodded, looking back at him.

Then Noureddine turned toward Anna and kissed her, forcing her down on the bed. Without any resistance on her part, Anna found herself being subtly seduced, her body being fondled and caressed by someone from whom she meant only to seek compassion and understanding. However, as Noureddine lowered his hand below her waist, Anna grabbed it in hers.

"No," she protested. "Don't do that."

"Why not?"

"Because it's not time," she explained. "You see, I wouldn't want to do anything just out of frustration or grief. I would want to do it only because I was ready for it."

Noureddine seemed a little disheartened by what he had just been told, but he still had to admit that Anna was right. "You've got a good point," he confessed. "Now is not the time, but I hope that someday it will be the right time for both of us."

"I do, too," Anna agreed.

The two of them stayed together the whole afternoon until Anna had gotten over the shock of what she had found out that morning. That evening, she thought as much about

Noureddine as she did about her brother. Now she knew that it was true. She was sure that it was not just a silly whim. The feeling was there—and it was real. It was a true passion that had developed from a simple friendship. Anna realized that this was what she both wanted and needed. But one thing she was not aware of was that her relationship with Noureddine was probably the only ray of hope that could help her cope with her coming, yet unfortunate fate.

By this time everybody at work was on Anna's back except for the other teachers in her department. Anna had to admit that, while her colleagues weren't exceptionally friendly to her, they at least didn't harass her as everybody else did. ("Everybody else" included the students, the administration, the coordinators and, of course, the director.) An even bigger problem was that by now, Anna had developed a reputation for being a born fumbler who couldn't do anything right, which in a way was true. In an environment such as that, nobody would have been able to do anything right.

One morning, as the mid-year exams were being given, Anna was approached by one of the members of the administration. This female coordinator was a loud-mouthed woman who made Anna wonder how she ever got the job, in a country where women were supposed to be so mild and soft-spoken. But it was not so much her robust personality that Anna found distasteful. It was the fact that she, among many others, went out of her way to give Anna a hard time.

That day the coordinator approached Anna in her usual tactless manner. "Miss Daleddo," she shouted as she walked up to her. "I understand that some of your classes' tests are missing."

"Yes," Anna retorted. "One group of them is already missing, and I've looked all over for them."

"Have you picked up your other exams yet?"

"No, I haven't. I was so busy looking for the exams that were lost that I haven't had time to get the other tests yet."

Then the coordinator looked at her with a most intimidating expression. "Now you're going to have to get them into the office of Monsieur le Directeur."

Monsieur le Directeur, Anna thought. Really, how could the woman get much nastier? She must have known that Anna was afraid of the director, and Anna was sure that she was doing it on purpose to put her on the spot.

"Listen," Anna said nervously. "How about if I get them and count them out on the secretary's desk right now?"

"All right," the coordinator consented. "But you'd better hurry if you don't want to see the director later on."

Oh, brother, Anna thought. Couldn't they leave her alone just this once? What was worse, Anna had a class that very minute, and she really needed to go right away. So there she was, trying to count out her exams and arrange them in a hurry so that she could go to her class. Yet even this she could not do without somebody else coming up to her and putting his two cents in. This time it was another coordinator, a younger fellow, who approached her.

"Miss Daleddo," he said, also sounding rather annoyed. "Your students are leaving. They're all going to cut your class in about a minute."

Anna, still trying to count out the tests, was practically frantic. She turned to the woman coordinator, who was still standing next to her. "Can't I do this later?" she pled. "Once I've finished all my classes?"

"Yes, you can," she replied coolly. "If you want to do it in the director's office."

Now Anna was irate. It was obvious that the coordinator was deliberately trying to back her into a corner and keep her there. So finally, after trying desperately to organize her exams, with little success, Anna decided to leave them there for the time being. To hell with it, she concluded. She felt that her students were her first priority and that now she must go to them. As she was leaving the secretary's desk, however, the director must have seen her from inside his office. Right before she went down to her class, she heard him yelling at her at the top of his lungs to get her exams together or get lost. Anna chose the latter.

Once she had finished her classes that morning, Anna reluctantly went back to the secretary's office. The strangest thing about the whole issue was that nobody said another word about it. The director and both the coordinators had apparently gone out for lunch. The secretary quite calmly gave Anna her exams, which she counted out and arranged right away. Also, the last set of tests that belonged to Anna was found and given back to her.

In spite of the fact that this ordeal had taken less than half an hour out of her day, Anna was aggravated. What were they all trying to prove? she asked. Deep inside, Anna realized that it was not the tests they were trying to keep up with. It was Anna herself. Increasingly, Anna was becoming aware that she was turning into a scapegoat for the frustration of everybody within the establishment, and more and more, she resented it. So immediately, she made up her mind that she was no longer going to take it lying down.

As Anna was leaving the Institute that afternoon, it happened that she ran into her favorite female coordinator. "Madame," she said as she walked up to her. "I don't know what all the confusion was about earlier today, but I'd like you to know that I got everything straightened out."

The coordinator gave Anna a sheepish look. "Oh," she said meekly. "I'm glad to hear that." Without saying another word, she walked away.

The next day would bring another unpleasant moment for Anna. It was the first time since she had been working there that she was to attend a faculty meeting with all the teachers of the English department. Needless to say, Anna didn't care to go, but she felt she had already gotten into enough trouble since she had been there, and she certainly had no need to tarnish her reputation any more. So Anna made up her mind that she would at least make her presence known at the conference.

At 3 p.m. all the members of the English department assembled in the teachers' room. Anna decided to camouflage herself at the corner of the large, executive-style table. That way, she felt she would be less noticed. The longer Anna was there, the more that uncomfortable, "out-of-place" feeling set in. Soon the director entered the room and sat at the head of the table, almost at the opposite end to where Anna was sitting. While all of the teachers had a briefcase full of documents or at least a folder in front of them, Anna had nothing. So before the meeting officially began, she hurried over to her small mailbox and got out a pen and some paper. By doing this, Anna thought that she would at least look professional.

The director commenced the meeting by discussing the importance of keeping track of tests once the students had completed and returned them for grading. He said that losing exams could cause a public scandal. Anna couldn't figure it, but she had to believe that the director knew what he was talking about. Still, during that time Anna got the feeling that she was the only person in the room besides the director. This is to say, it seemed as if the director was talking only to her. The reason was that, when it was discovered that some of the tests were lost, Anna seemed to be the only one to get any flack about it. There must have been other teachers who were missing exams, she thought. Furthermore, once these exams were completed by the students, they were not returned directly to their teachers. Instead, they went through several channels before they were graded. So wasn't this just as much the responsibility of the administration as it was the teachers? Oh, well. Anna knew that she was in no position to argue with anybody in that establishment.

Anna soon shook out of her daze and returned her attention to what the director was presently talking about. He went on to discuss the curriculum for the second half of the school year and future testing procedures. The whole meeting didn't last long—a half hour, forty-five minutes at the most. As far as Anna was concerned, it was an extreme waste of time. As always, the director didn't accomplish anything concrete or lasting. Instead, he just complained and preferred to leave any possible solutions for such problems to his subordinates. Some overseer, Anna thought.

As Anna was leaving the Institute that day, she felt that she had been nothing more than a bump on a log at that meeting. Except for just the appearance of it, she figured she didn't even have any business being there. But this didn't surprise her, as she had assumed that all along. Anna knew that she had so much more to offer than anybody there gave her credit for. One of these days, she thought, she would prove it.

One of the most obvious problems Anna might have expected in a country like Tunisia was a considerable amount of male harassment. This indeed turned out to be an understatement. There were two major reasons for this. One was that most Tunisian women did not parade around alone as Anna did, even during the day. The other was that Anna, being fair-skinned, was noticeably a foreigner. Even though Anna had anticipated this, her patience was already wearing a bit thin. It seemed that almost every time she went outside, she could not avoid being followed by some gallant suitor who was obviously looking to show her a good time.

One afternoon when Anna had some shopping to do near the main avenue, she left the Institute with the intention of taking a walk to the center of town. A young man whom she had seen before soon spotted her and wasted no time in joining her in her brief excursion. Anna started walking faster, but it did no good. He did everything he could to keep up with her pace. Then she tried to ignore his verbal approaches, hoping that this would offer him some discouragement, but again, it didn't do much good. He just kept pestering her and didn't seem to care much if he was getting a response or not.

When Anna arrived at the department store where she wanted to shop, she thought for sure that this fine gentleman would at last bug off, but it never happened. Not only did he enter the store with her, he then proceeded to follow her up to the second floor. At this point everybody was beginning to notice what was going on, but this still did not deter the man from pursuing Anna. At this moment, Anna thought she would take advantage of a golden opportunity.

"Look, buddy," she said. "I want to make one thing clear right now. That is that I'm not going to go out with you." But the man continued to follow her as she browsed in the store, so Anna turned to him again, this time sounding a bit more forceful. "And another thing. I'm not going to have sex with you!"

Everybody stopped and stared. This was just the reaction Anna wanted. Even she was smiling. She hoped that her gentleman friend was happy that he had attracted so much attention. Once the crowd had died down and went on its way, the man went up to her, this time in a more private fashion.

"I'd like to know what you meant by that comment," he said.

Anna turned to the man one more time. "All I meant was that if somebody isn't interested in you, it's not worth your trouble to go on a hot pursuit as you were doing. After all, you're wasting your time as well as mine."

The man acted like he felt a little foolish, and he finally walked away and eventually went downstairs again. Anna, in turn, did her shopping and then left the store as well.

As Anna was walking home, she reflected on what had happened that day. Presumably, she'd had all she could take of this kind of adulation. But what she did took nerve, she thought. And she was in a Moslem country, no less. That would teach them to try to censure Anna, as she definitely had a mind of her own and was never short of tricks up her sleeve. So what Anna did made her feel assertive and force-ful—emotions she had not experienced in a long time. And the irony was that Anna went ahead and did it in a country where women were supposed to be mild and soft-spoken.

Despite the fact that everybody at work was out to tor-ment Anna to death, she was determined not to let such bureaucratic nonsense affect her personal life. If everyone within the administration was out to dump their own responsibility in Anna's lap, she wasn't about to take it home with her. So she didn't. There, she had her own life—one that consisted of friendship and love.

Tonight was very special for Anna. Now she was finally ready to consummate her relationship with Noured-dine. She was now sure beyond a shadow of a doubt that she loved Noureddine and that she wanted to make love to him. Anna also knew that later on, there would be no compro-mise or regret.

This evening Anna was unusually calm as she waited for Noureddine to come to her apartment. She felt neither anxious nor tense. The way she perceived it was that love should only come out of sincere desire. It should never be forced, as if the feeling were lacking or as if it weren't there from the very start. For her, love needed to be completely natural and spontaneous. If not, it wouldn't take place at all. So Anna knew that whatever happened that night was sim-ply meant to be.

Soon enough, the doorbell rang. Anna, who was lying on her bed, got up quietly and walked out of her room. She turned the light on in the hallway before she went up to the door. When she opened it, she found Noureddine standing there.

"Hi," she greeted him.

"Hello," he replied. Then Noureddine walked in and went directly into Anna's room, with Anna following him to the door.

"Want something to drink?" she asked, now standing by her bedroom door.

"What have you got?" Noureddine inquired as he sat down on a desk chair.

"How about some wine?" Anna suggested, as if that were what she had planned all along.

"OK," Noureddine agreed. Then Anna left the room.

When she came back, she was holding two glasses of red wine. "Here," she said, handing one to him as she sat on the bed facing him. Then she looked at Noureddine with a subtle smile on her face. "How have you been?" she asked him.

"I've been fine," he answered. "But what's with you? Why are you smiling like that?"

"I'm just happy, I suppose."

"Are you sure you don't have something up your sleeve?" Noureddine challenged her. "You're acting a little too happy tonight."

"Drink your wine," she advised him, as she sipped on her own glass. "We'll talk about it later."

Without saying anything to Noureddine, she turned off the desk lamp and lit a candle on her night table. Noureddine said nothing to Anna as he went over and lay down on her bed. Anna, still sitting on the edge of the bed, turned toward Noureddine. They both had their wine glasses in their hands, but Noureddine set his glass on the night table and lit up a cigarette.

There was no speech, no discussion, no "talking about it later," as Anna had referred to it earlier. Somehow, though, they were relating their feelings to each other. They both knew what they wanted, and they knew what was happening. With no resistance to the apparent temptation, Noureddine put his cigarette in an ashtray on the night table, reached up and pulled open a bow that Anna had tied in her lace blouse. With that hint, Anna slowly unbuttoned her blouse, taking it completely off. Then Noureddine reached around under her arms and unhooked her bra. Slowly Anna's breasts were exposed as he pulled the undergarment away from her body. Then Anna unzipped her denim skirt and pulled it down, along with her stockings, over her legs and off her feet. Then she removed her underpants, so that now she was completely nude.

Surprisingly enough, Anna was more self conscious about seeing Noureddine undress than she was about exposing her own body. She lay on the bed, completely nude, as Noureddine undressed, but she did not look up at him as he did so. When Noureddine had completely disrobed, he climbed into bed and got under the covers. Then Anna did the same.

For the first time since they had met, Anna was the one who was far more passionate. She circled her arms around Noureddine's shoulders as she moved her body on top of his. Then she pulled up her knees and placed them around his torso. She leaned her body close to his as he penetrated her. Anna gasped with intense excitement as she felt the most heightened sensations she had ever experienced. And when they both climaxed, they let out a simultaneous cry of joy and satisfaction. Once Noureddine had calmed down, Anna slowly and cautiously lifted her body off his and lay down next to him.

Anna lay there for a few moments, reflecting on what had just transpired. Then she turned around, only to find that her lover was almost asleep. "Noureddine," Anna whispered.

"Hum?" he responded.

"How about if you spend the night?"

The next morning Anna and Noureddine both slept very late. Anna was the first to wake up. She tossed and turned for quite a while before she finally opened her eyes. Then immediately, she looked beside her to find that Noureddine was still sound asleep. He was, in fact, lying very, very still.

As it was already late morning, the sunlight was streaming through the window in rays that looked almost like a rainbow. The whole scene was like a beautiful picture to Anna—it all seemed so fitting after what she had experienced the night before. She was, in fact, so satisfied that she had not even the desire to disturb the peaceful rest of Noureddine. So rather than wake him up, she just lay there, pondering over her new and blossoming relationship.

Soon, though, Noureddine began to wake up, shifting his body slowly so that he was now lying on his back. Then finally, his eyes flickered open. He turned toward Anna and glanced at her.

"Good morning," he said.

"Hi." Not knowing what else to do, she decided to offer him some breakfast. "Want some coffee?"

"Yes, I do," he said, sounding somewhat preoccupied. As Anna proceeded to get out of bed, however, she was quickly stopped by Noureddine, who grabbed her by the arm. "Annie," he said, "tell me one thing before you go. Who was it?"

Anna turned and looked at him. "Who was what?" she challenged him. "What are you talking about?"

"Don't play dumb with me," he said. "You know what I'm talking about. Who was it who had you before I did?"

Anna couldn't believe her ears. "What's it to you?" she argued. "Did you actually expect me to be chaste before you got to me?"

"No, I didn't," he declared. "I just want to know who it was, that's all." Noureddine's manner of speaking was curt and inquisitive.

"Do you have to ask me in that tone of voice?" she scolded him. "Frankly, I don't think it's any of your business anyway."

"What?" Noureddine replied. "Are you ashamed of your past experiences?"

"Why should I be?" Anna asked. "I just don't feel like telling you about them. Like I said, it shouldn't matter to you anyway."

"Then don't tell me," Noureddine conceded. "But that way I'll always be wondering. I'll never be sure about you, Annie."

Now Anna was furious. Who was he to ask her about her previous experiences, especially when he was asking about it in such a provocative manner? But on the other hand, Anna needed to recognize the kind of background Noureddine was from and that the question of chastity was much more important to him than it was to her. So finally she gave in.

"All right," she concluded. "If you must know, I'll tell you. Last year and not until last year, I met a man, and I made love to him, and that was it."

"That was it?" Noureddine questioned her. "You just made love to him for its own sake?"

"Of course not," Anna said. "I did it because I loved him."

"Then why aren't you still together today?"

"Because it was just a summer romance," Anna explained. "Neither one of us wanted anything more permanent, so when I went away, we just ended it."

"What do you mean when you say that neither one of you wanted anything more permanent?" Noureddine inquired.

"I guess I mean that neither one of us were thinking in terms of marriage," Anna shrugged. "I guess we just weren't ready for it."

"If you were really in love, why weren't you ready for it?"

"Noureddine," Anna said. "You don't have to be ready for marriage to be in love with somebody. Sometimes the circumstances don't work out right for marriage."

Noureddine looked hurt. "I never looked at it that way," he said. "To me, it's just that if you really loved somebody, you would want to get married regardless of the circumstances."

Even though what he was saying didn't make much sense to Anna, she couldn't help but feel guilty when she saw Noureddine's reaction to what she was telling him. "Noureddine," she said again. "I know that your beliefs are very different from mine, but can't you see that what happened last year is over and that it doesn't matter anyway?"

"I guess so," Noureddine agreed. "But I just can't help thinking about it, that's all."

While Noureddine still acted preoccupied about what they had just been discussing, Anna seemed equally and clearly preoccupied about another matter. Now she was lying back on her bed, staring thoughtfully up at the ceiling. Seeing that she looked troubled, Noureddine turned toward her.

"What's the matter, Annie?" he asked her. "What's on your mind?"

"Oh, I'm thinking about my brother," she sighed. "I'm so damned selfish, you know. Here I am, almost at the other side of the world. Actually, when you think of where he is, I really should be there."

Chapter 7

There were two main wards at the Carolina State Hospital—one for the physically sick, and one for the mentally ill. For space and security reasons, the patients were kept in totally separate buildings. Only one was locked up. The patients with physical ailments could come and go as they pleased. Those with mental disorders could only leave with special passes. Paul Daleddo, unfortunately, was not nearly up to that level.

Today was one of those days when Paul had to be restrained. There he lay in a padded cell, wrapped in a straitjacket, squirming and twitching all over. His arms were crossed over his stomach, his hands belted from the back. He was on the floor, lying on his side, with his legs curled up almost to his chest. He was wearing a white pajama-type suit—typical of what they always gave to mental patients.

Now Paul was unimaginably overwrought and fatigued. Drops of sweat trickled from his forehead, and his hairline was completely wet. There were noticeable circles around his eyes, most probably from lack of sleep. Yet to this day, his complexion was perfect. There were absolutely no wounds or scratch marks on his body. His physique still looked slender and trim. His hair was golden brown, and his hazel eyes glowed. One could say that Paul was still the handsome boy he had been all his life.

Now, though, Paul jerked his body back and forth. Yet it did not seem as if he were struggling to get free. It appeared more as if he was simply moving his body in a perpetual and uncontrollable manner. While Paul seemed completely unaware of his surroundings, nothing could have been further from the truth. On the contrary, he was very aware of his surroundings, and he was suffering terribly. He wanted so much to get out of his imprisonment, but how could he, when he had absolutely no control over his own body movements?

How long had Paul been inside this padded chamber? Who knows? He could have been there for hours. And why on earth had they put him there? Perhaps because he'd had had a fit or tantrum that morning. In Paul's present state of torment, this was a very real possibility. The guards kept close watch on the patients to make sure that they didn't hurt themselves or each other through any act of violence. So maybe one of the hospital attendants had put him there. Alas, it was this possibility that turned out to be true.

When somebody finally came to let Paul out, it was already early afternoon. Yet it was still dark in the room, since it was closed in on all sides. At last, though, the huge iron door opened slowly, letting the light angle in from the next room. The light grew brighter as the door opened wider. And there, outside the door, stood a guard waiting to let Paul out.

"OK, Paul," he said agreeably. "Let's go."

Once the door had opened completely, the guard bent down to his knees behind Paul, untied the straitjacket from the back, and took it off. Then he gently put his arms around Paul's chest and helped him to his feet. Paul seemed temporarily paralyzed, his arms hanging limply from his sides. As much as he tried to stand up on his own, he would have fallen flat on his face without the guard's support. The guard took Paul's arm and put it around his shoulders and carefully helped him out of the cell.

Once they had arrived at Paul's room, the guard reached for a large keychain attached to his belt. Finding the key and opening the door with one hand, he led Paul inside. Paul staggered over to his bed, lay down, and with the help of the guard, was covered with the sheets. Now Paul seemed considerably more at ease, despite his present condition, as he was obviously more comfortable lying in his bed than when he was in that cell.

The guard stood up and reached into his pocket. He pulled out a syringe and rubber strap used to restrict the blood flow of the veins. He removed the cap which covered the needle of the syringe. Still holding the needle, he tied the strap around Paul's upper arm. Locating Paul's principal vein, the guard carefully inserted the needle into Paul's arm. Barely conscious, Paul only flinched a bit from the pain of the injection. The guard then removed the needle, covered it with the cap again, and shoved it into his pocket. He untied the arm-band and disposed of it. As soon as he saw that Paul was settled and quiet, the guard bent over the bed and spoke softly to him.

"Paul," he whispered. "I don't want to see any more of what was going on this morning. If you continue to carry on like that, you'll have to be sedated even more than usual, and you won't be let out of your room at all. Is that clear?"

Paul turned his head slightly, as if nodding. Since the guard knew that Paul had caught on to what he was saying, he got up and walked over to the door. He opened it, but before he left, he turned around one last time.

"Sleep well, Paul," he told him. Then the guard closed the door quietly, locking it securely from the outside.

Paul had been sleeping for at least eighteen hours over the past day and night, by the time his parents came to see him at the hospital the next morning. Around 8 a.m. Robert and Louis Daleddo, accompanied by the head of the psychiatric ward at the Carolina State Hospital, Dr. James Stanton, walked into his room. Paul did not appear to be least bit disturbed by their entrance. Because he had been given several sedatives during the night, he was asleep. The doctor smiled when he saw Paul sleeping so peacefully, although he realized that he would soon have to wake him up.

Stanton went to the bed and tapped Paul lightly on the shoulder. Paul twitched a little, showing no real response. It was obvious that he was still fast asleep, so the doctor had to become a bit more assertive.

"Paul," he insisted. "It's time to wake up. There are some people here to see you." There was still no response

When Paul refused to wake up with a little more encouragement, the doctor felt he had to get quite a bit more forceful. He took Paul by the arm and pulled him up to a sitting position. Then he pulled his legs out from under the covers and placed them over the side of the bed, turning Paul slightly around. Even though he knew what was going on, Paul just slouched over, still depending on the doctor to hold him up straight.

"Come on," said Stanton. "I know you want to get out of here sooner or later. So let's go." He took Paul's arm and put it around his shoulder, helped him out of bed, and led him to the door. Once the doctor and Paul had left the room together, both his parents walked out as well.

The doctor, Paul, and his parents all went to the visitors' lounge, where there were some comfortable sofas and chairs to relax and stretch out on. Robert and Louise sat in two upholstered chairs, while their son was placed on the sofa. As always, Paul had to be carefully supported by the doctor to make sure he didn't collapse on the floor.

Paul was wide awake. In his current natural state, although he could see or hear everything going on around him, he was unable to respond. Because of the medication he was taking as a relaxant, Paul had little control over his body movements. He could not speak, eat, or stand up on his own. Even when he looked at his parents, it was as if he saw right through them. Yet he didn't. He was simply unable to react to them.

Needless to say, Paul's condition affected his parents. At times they didn't know what to do when they saw him. If they tried to talk to him, they knew he wouldn't say anything back. If they offered him something, he wouldn't know how to take it. If they tried to touch him, they were afraid he might physically reject them. So instead, they just sat and stared at Paul, feeling as if they could do nothing for him. Fortunately, though, the psychiatrist knew when to call the visit to an end.

"I think it's time for Paul to go back to his room," he suggested. "He hasn't eaten anything today, you know." The doctor turned and looked at Robert and Louise. "You can go to my office and wait there while I take him back." As before, Paul got up with the psychiatrist's help and staggered out the door. The Daleddos followed.

They waited at least twenty minutes in Stanton's office while the doctor took care of Paul. Finally, he came back. He greeted them both pleasantly as he sat down at his desk. "I'm sorry I took so long," he apologized. "But it was necessary that Paul have some breakfast. He doesn't eat anything unless he's obliged to do so."

When they heard this, Robert and Louise acted even more disheartened. Obviously, Stanton had a lot of experience in dealing with the parents of mentally ill patients. Since it was a delicate matter, he knew that there were things to say and things not to say. However, the doctor was well aware of the fact that he must never lie or distort the truth to the parents.

"There's no doubt about it," Stanton admitted. "Your son is in a very serious state. He has had a major breakdown."

"What exactly does that mean, doctor?" Louise asked.

"It means that an exact analysis of his condition has not yet been made, as he has been here for less than a month.

But as far as the degree of his condition goes, it is quite severe."

"But why?" Robert challenged him. "Why did all this happen?"

"Mr. Daleddo," Stanton said calmly. "I know only what you told me. You said that shortly after he went back to his job in North Carolina, he broke down completely. It is my opinion that he experienced the breakdown when he was still at home. The fact that he had to go back to Greensboro alone makes it appear to have happened at that time."

This made the Daleddos feel all the more guilty. Had they driven Paul into this state because they let him go back to his job—or was he already there anyway? After all, Stanton must know what he was talking about.

"Dr. Stanton," Louise said, "you say that Paul's condition had been building for a long time. Could you be a little more specific about that?"

"It is very hard to pinpoint exactly where it started. I'm going strictly by what you told me. You say that Paul was very troubled at his first job and instead of telling you this, he went on to accept a position which was even more demanding. By the time you realized this, it was too late. Paul was already in the state of panic and disorientation."

Panic and disorientation, the Daleddos thought. That was putting it mildly. They were obviously displeased by such ambiguity. As their anxiety was somewhat understandable to the doctor, he felt that a further explanation was in order.

"I think you both should know exactly what Paul's status is at this time," Stanton explained. "Right now, Paul will be strictly supervised until he displays more compatible behavior. When this occurs, he will be given more and more freedom, until he will eventually be let out of the hospital. During this time, he will be taking medication regularly."

"How much longer will he have to stay here?" Robert inquired.

"Oh," Stanton sighed. "I should think that he'll have to remain committed for a while longer. I would say for at least a couple of months."

"A couple of months!" Robert exclaimed. (Judging by his reaction, one would have thought that the doctor had said that Paul had to remain there for a couple of years.) "Can't he get out sooner?"

"Please, people," Stanton begged. "Let's play it by ear. When Paul is ready to leave as an outpatient, I'll let you know. Meanwhile, if you so desire, you can come over to see your son from time to time."

"Oh, we're planning to come over to see him every weekend until he gets better," Robert promised.

"That's very considerate of both of you," Stanton commended them.

Then the three of them rose from their seats and went to the door. "I just wanted to say one more thing, Mr. and Mrs. Daleddo," the doctor added. "Your son has a very good chance of recovery and a good opportunity to lead to a normal life afterward. It takes a little time and patience, that's all."

Once Robert and Louise had thanked the doctor, they left the office together. They walked down the hall to a nearby elevator. As they were rode down to the first floor, Louise suddenly broke down and started sobbing. This type of behavior was rare for her these days, as most of the time she felt too desperate to express her feelings so freely. When he saw how upset his wife had become, Robert leaned toward her, putting his arm around her shoulders.

"It's all right, Louise," he assured her. "There's no need to worry about it anymore."

When the door to the elevator opened, they both walked out.

The Daleddos spent the whole afternoon resting in their hotel room. It was now early evening. The television was on, and the lights were low. Louise, now more composed, was relaxing on the bed. Robert, meanwhile, was in the bathroom washing up.

"You know," Louise said to her husband. "I don't know where we went wrong. I don't know where we failed Paul."

Robert, with his sleeves rolled up, was still facing the sink. "I don't either," he said. "I honestly don't."

"They say that mental illness comes from a troubled background, but this one I can't figure out."

"Neither can I," Robert said. "Really, I can't."

Robert and Louise had never been separated since their wedding. They had never had any serious behavior problems with either of their children, and neither of them had been deprived physically or materially. Since her two children were born, Louise had never worked or done anything to cause her to neglect them. Robert had always had a stable if not prestigious job and was always a steady provider. Nevertheless, mental illness always traces its way back to the family background, and Robert and Louise could not forget that. As a result, Paul's parents loaded themselves down with guilt because of what had happened to their son.

Once Robert had finished washing up, he turned off the light in the bathroom, went to the bedroom, sat down on the other side of the bed, and stretched out. Louise reached up and flicked off the light switch above her, so that the only light in the room was from the television. Having nothing else to say or do, the Daleddos watched TV.

A little more than a month had passed. Paul had made tremendous progress. It was getting to the point where he almost always talked logically and was psychologically responsive and physically independent. He was no longer under close observation and was free to go anywhere he wanted within that section of the hospital. He also needed little help to get around and do things for himself.

It was hard to tell why Paul had made so much progress in so short a time. Perhaps it was because this was an exceptionally good hospital with an exceptionally good staff. It was also possible that the medication that Paul was taking had a positive effect on him. But Paul attributed most of his progress to the care and attention his parents had given him while he was in the hospital. As Robert said, every weekend they drove all the way from Baltimore to Greensboro and back just to see their son. While with him, they were supportive of him in his condition, keeping close track of what he was doing and eager to find how they could help him. They also saw Stanton and the other members of the staff regularly to make sure that they were offering as much assistance as they possibly could to help bring about Paul's recovery.

At the same time, though, Paul was still a depressed young man. He showed little enthusiasm. He rarely spoke unless he was spoken to, and his once outstanding personality was almost nonexistent. He had to be heavily sedated, giving him a somewhat sluggish appearance and making his movements rather awkward and uncoordinated. Nevertheless, Paul's medication had been reduced to the point where he could do almost anything on his own.

Paul had been in that special ward for about two months. During this time, he had seen nothing of the outside world, except for the grounds and gardens of the hospital. However, Paul had improved so much that Stanton finally consented to let him out earlier than they all had expected. So there Paul was, in regular clothes, which he hadn't worn since he was admitted to that ward such a long time ago. He was sitting on the edge of his bed, his suitcase beside him on the floor, waiting for his parents to come pick him up.

Soon Paul's parents came into the room, this time accompanied by one of the attendants. "Come on, Paul," the attendant said. "It's time to go."

Paul showed little reaction. Finally he took a deep breath and got up listlessly from the bed. He picked up his suitcase, walked slowly to the door, and all four of them left the room together. They took the elevator to the ground floor, and once they had arrived at the main entrance door, the attendant left them there. Paul and his parents went out of the hospital alone.

When they got outside, the three of them walked to the parking lot and went to Robert's car. Before he got in, however, Paul took one last look at that huge brick building in which he had been imprisoned for so long. Good riddance, he declared. Farewell—and never again. Then he got into the back seat of the car, while his father put his suitcase in the trunk. Once they were all settled in, Robert started up the car and pulled out of the parking lot.

After they were out on the main highway, Louise attempted to start a casual conversation. "So, Paul," she addressed him. "How does it feel to be out?"

"Great," he said half-heartedly. He didn't say anything more.

Chapter 8

As soon as their son was out of the hospital, the Daleddos were as anxious as Paul was to see things return to normal. They were so anxious, in fact, that they wanted to erase everything from their minds that had happened to Paul since he left his computer sales job at Mackenfield. But when Robert and Louise returned to Baltimore, they found that this task would be more difficult than they had expected. Paul's parents had not been home for even three full days when they received an intriguing, yet disturbing letter from the Greenboro Branch of Mackenfield, Inc.

Robert was the first to see the letter. Even though it was addressed to Paul, he took the liberty of opening it. He figured that if it was more bad news, he would want to be the first one to know about it. And, indeed, it was.

When Robert opened the envelope and unfolded the letter, there was a brief and insensitive note referring to Paul's status of employment. It read as follows:

Paul Daleddo: TERMINATED.

The date appeared on the next line, followed by the name and signature of the executive director of the company.

Robert could feel his temperature rise. The nerve of these people, he thought. They fired his son without even telling Paul to his face. When Robert told Louise about the letter, she was as upset as he was. While they tried to excuse it as the action of impersonal and unfeeling bureaucrats, they could not get it out of their minds. Finally, after a few days of dwelling on it, they decided to go back to North Carolina and pay this supervisor of Paul's a visit.

Once in Greensboro, the Daleddos went directly to the office building where Paul had worked. When they saw the size of a single branch of this establishment, they were impressed and could understand why Paul had been so proud and elated to be an employee there. At the same time, though, they have found the whole scenario very depressing, as all this was certainly a thing of the past.

Robert and Louise had an old business card of Paul's with them. They went directly to the fifth floor and located Milsten's office right away. When they went in, they found the same secretary who had worked with Paul. She smiled to see two newcomers walking in the door.

"Hello," she greeted them. "May I help you?"

"Yes, you may," Robert said. "We'd like to see Mr. Milsten."

"Who should I say is asking for him?"

"Robert and Louise Daleddo."

The woman's pleasant expression changed to one of extreme anxiety. "Oh," she said, almost cringing. "I'll see if he's available."

She picked up the phone and dialed Milsten's extension. "Mr. Milsten," she said quietly, holding the receiver close to her mouth. "Mr. and Mrs. Daleddo are here to see you." She hesitated for a few seconds. "OK," she replied. The secretary hung up the phone and looked at Robert and Louise. "Mr. Milsten will be out shortly."

Not long after the Daleddos sat down in the waiting room, a man came out of his office and into the waiting room. "Hi," he said, smiling. "Would you like to follow me back to my office?" Robert and Louise nodded as they got up from their seats, and all three of them went back together.

Once they had entered Milsten's plush executive office, he closed the door and went behind his desk. "You must be Paul Daleddo's parents," he said, extending his hand to Louise first.

"Yes, we are," Louise responded, shaking Milsten's hand. Then Robert did the same.

"Henry Milsten," he said. All three of them sat down. "What can I do for you people today?" Paul's former boss was as casual and laid back as ever.

"My wife and I need a bit of clarification regarding our son, Paul." Robert began. "We understand that he used to work under you."

"That is correct," Milsten said, without a flicker of emotion showing on his face.

"We received a letter that stated plainly that Paul was terminated from his job here. Do you know anything about that correspondence?"

"Yes, I do. As a matter of fact, I was the one who put the termination notice into effect." Milsten was as stiff as a piece of lumber, showing no feelings of guilt or remorse about what he was saying.

"But why?" Louise questioned. "Why did you do it? And why didn't you at least contact our son first?"

"Mrs. Daleddo," Milsten addressed her. "As I understand it, when Paul discovered that he wasn't going to make it at this job, he had a very serious breakdown. We also found out that he had been hospitalized for some time. Isn't that true?"

"Yes," Robert admitted. "It is true."

"So how do you expect me to keep somebody on in that condition? If he wasn't successful before this happened to him, things certainly wouldn't improve for him afterward. So, for the sake of your son as well as for the company, I recommended to the executive director that Paul be terminated. And as far as Paul being contacted about it goes, the letter was addressed to him, wasn't it?"

Now it was Louise's turn to act sheepish. "Yes, it was," she said. "We just read it first."

Then Robert abruptly interrupted. "So are you saying that Paul will not be returning to this job?"

Milsten sighed as he sat back in his chair. "Let me answer your question with a question. Would your son want to come back? Would he even be comfortable returning here after all that he's been through?"

Robert looked down instead of at Milsten. "No, I suppose not," he said.

The Daleddos didn't know what to say next. Deep inside, they both knew that Milsten was right, even though they felt he could have been a little more compassionate about it. After all, this was their son they were talking about, not some robot who could simply be dismantled and tossed aside. When Milsten saw how hurt Robert and Louise appeared to be, he softened his tone.

"I want you to understand, Mr. and Mrs. Daleddo, that nobody knows more than I do how difficult this kind of work is. As a matter of fact, there was a time that I, too, was close to a breakdown. Fortunately, I got through it without that happening."

"Thank you for telling us that," Louise told him. "We appreciate your support."

As the Daleddos rose from their seats, so did Milsten. He accompanied them to the door and looked at Robert and Louise one more time. "I want you to know one thing," he said. "I think that your son has a good chance of recovery and an excellent chance to lead to a normal life. It just takes time, that's all."

After the Daleddos thanked Milsten for seeing them, they left his office. On their way out of the building and into the parking lot, Paul's parents thought about that last statement Milsten had made about their son having such a "good chance for recovery" and for a "normal life." They had heard that line somewhere before. Was it even true? They really wondered. At any rate, the Daleddos got what they had come there for—information about their son. As soon as Robert and Louise found their car, they got inside and drove away.

When Paul had returned home from the hospital, he elected to stay at his house in Baltimore rather than going back to North Carolina. There were two basic reasons for this decision: one, the employment situation was considerably better in Baltimore than it was in Greensboro; and two, his house in Greensboro had too many depressing memories of what had happened to him before his breakdown. Even so, what Paul did not take into consideration was that wherever he went, his problems would follow him.

Staying at his parents' home, Paul was about as apathetic as he had been when he was in the hospital. As an outpatient, he was still obligated to take quite a bit of medication, which left him feeling drowsy and lethargic. So now Paul spent most of his time lying around the house, sleeping, eating, or watching television. He didn't go out much, and he hardly ever mixed with other people.

As time went on, however, Paul's condition began to change, but not in a stable sense. His behavior became less consistent and more erratic. On some days he would show incredible sparks of enthusiasm; on others he was the same as before. Again, it was difficult to determine why Paul's behavior was changing in the way it was. The most likely reason was that Paul was reacting to the effects of his medicine with extreme moodiness. The medication was not able to create an adequate balance within Paul's system, and as a result, he was not able to maintain an even temperament. Yet despite the fact that these frequent changes in disposition were not a realistic way to measure Paul's progress, the days when he felt good encouraged both of his parents, exciting them so much that they actually believed that their son had completely recovered.

One morning Paul woke up rather early, got hold of a newspaper and began to look for ads offering employment. He scanned over that whole section of the paper until he found something that looked interesting:

"National Exchange, Inc. wants manager to handle clientele matters and credit issues."

This is the job for me, Paul concluded. It'll be easy by comparison with what I was doing before. All I have to do is tell them that I was a manager at Steamers and Mackenfield when I was working there.

Naturally, this final statement was nothing short of a lie. Paul was a low man at both the companies where he had previously worked. So now he was looking to be a manager? Not to mention that experience in computer sales had little to do with credit issues. Even so, Paul was determined to give them that line.

Paul picked up the phone and dialed the number given there in the newspaper. The telephone on the other end of the line rang several times before someone finally came and answered it. At least Paul's call had a reply.

"Hello?" he said in an excited voice. "Yeah, I'm calling about your ad in the newspaper for a credit manager...Yeah, I've had experience. I was a sales manager at two computer companies...Steamers and Mackenfield...Yes, that's right, Mackenfield...OK, then, I'll see you in about an hour. Goodbye!" In a flash he hung up the phone.

Paul ran to his room and started getting dressed. His mother was still in bed trying to sleep. When she heard all this commotion, she got up and went to her bedroom door.

"Paul," she called. "What's going on?"

"I'm going for an interview," he shouted from his room.

"An interview for what?"

"For a job."

"A job? Where?"

"National Exchange."

"Oh. Good luck, then." Louise closed the door and went back to bed.

Paul was ecstatic. He believed that he was coming up in the world again. He knew he was going to get this job, no matter what he had to do. Little did he know that lying to get the job would not turn out to be worth it.

Leaving the house that morning, Paul as zippy as when he was still working at Mackenfield. Louise went out to do some shopping and then went to have lunch at the restaurant where she usually ate at that hour, whether she was alone or with her children. She was sitting in one of the booths with a cup of coffee and newspaper in front of her when, to her total surprise, Paul came rushing in the door of the restaurant, looking outrageously happy.

"Congratulate me, Mom," he greeted her. "I got the job."

Louise gasped. "You did?"

"I sure did," Paul said. "I am a credit manager at National Exchange, Inc."

"You certainly deserve to be congratulated," Louise commended him. "Let me treat you to lunch."

The next week Paul started his new job. His parents were overjoyed about the whole idea. What they did not realize was that their son had lied to get the job. They also did not take into consideration that such responsibilities for Paul would be a bit too much too soon.

The first day when he went to work, Paul seemed exceptionally excited about it. Yet when he arrived at the building where he would soon start working, he saw that it wasn't a tenth the size of the Mackenfield branch in Greensboro. This new place was located in a small office building in the heart of Baltimore City. Inside, Paul found that the place was clean, modern, and looked recently renovated.

Although it appeared to be a dinky old building on the outside, on the inside it looked to be quite up to date.

The first thing for Paul to do was to go upstairs to meet his new employer. This was the director of the Baltimore branch of National Exchange, Inc. So Paul took the stairs up to the second floor and went immediately to the director's office.

"Hello," Paul greeted the man as he entered his office. "You told me to come in today."

The director, sitting at his desk, looked content enough to see Paul. "Oh, yes," he smiled. "You're the young man who was hired last week. Your name is Paul, isn't it?"

"Yes," he said. "I'm Paul Daleddo." When Paul approached his desk, the director stood up formally to shake his hand.

"William Haller," he said as he introduced himself. "Please do sit down." Paul sat in one of the armchairs in front of the director while Haller sat back down at his desk. "I understand that you've had managerial experience, Paul."

"Yes, I have," Paul stated.

"Good, because that's what we're looking for here. I guess you can start out by meeting your staff."

"My staff?" Paul echoed. He was already getting scared.

"Yes, your staff," he repeated. "The people who will be working under you."

"How many people are there under me?" he asked nervously.

"Oh, not that many," Haller commented. "Altogether there are eleven people."

Paul felt a cold chill run down his spine. Oh, God, he thought. Eleven people are eleven too many. How could he possibly hack it when he didn't know what he was doing in the first place? Paul knew all too well that he had never done this type of work before in his life. Oh, well, he concluded. Paul realized that he would have to go ahead with his plan, as now it was far too late to back out.

"OK," he said. "I'd be happy to meet my new crew." Then Paul and Haller went downstairs together.

The main office where Paul's staff was working looked something like a bank. There were office windows, in front of which people stood in line to take care of their loans and debts. Many of the men and women there working under Paul looked quite a bit older than he did. Some seemed to be middle aged. This made Paul nervous, as he was not used to supervising anybody, let alone people who were twenty years older than he was. At any rate, when Paul saw who he would be working with and what everybody was doing, a cold chill went through him again.

Paul and Haller stood and observed for a while what was going on in the main office. They just stayed there and watched so that Paul could see what everyone was doing. When noon rolled around and there were no more customers in the office, Haller called all the employees over in a group.

"Ladies and gentlemen," he announced. "I would like you to meet your new supervisor, Paul Daleddo. From now on, Mr. Daleddo will be handling all the credit and clientele matters. So if there are any problems of this nature, go see him about them."

Oh, God, Paul thought again, Credit and clientele problems? He knew absolutely nothing on the subject. How was he supposed to take care of these kinds of issues, when he didn't even know what they were? Somehow, Paul couldn't help but feel as if he had been thrown into a river and were drowning in it. But good, bad, or indifferent, he would begin working that very day.

Paul really didn't know what to do with himself while he was there, so he started by walking around to each of the windows to see what the employees were doing. Some were checking out credit records, some were taking in money and handing out receipts, and some were handling money withdrawals and giving them out to the customers. Paul didn't understand half of what was going on. He was supposed to take care of any customer complaints that should arise? Ugh, he remarked to himself. Paul could not wait for that.

By that afternoon, the office was packed again. The more people Paul saw come in, the worse he felt. He was literally getting sick to his stomach. The noise and commotion, along with the medication he was taking, was making him terribly nauseous. It even got to the point where Paul was afraid of fainting. To make matters worse, he had not even been assigned office space yet, so there was no place for him to sit down.

Around three in the afternoon, Paul got his first customer complaint. A woman who appeared to be in her mid-fifties went up to one of the windows that handled debts and returns. It seemed that this lady owed some money on a loan that had been issued to her with interest. The attendant at the window appeared to be a young man, looking to be not much older than Paul. The disagreement between the two of them occurred when the man handed the customer back her payment book and told her how much money she owed. The woman shouted out so loud that everybody in the office must have heard her.

"What?" she exclaimed. "I don't owe you that much."

"I'm sorry, ma'am," he apologized. "But you were given the loan at five percent interest."

"No," she insisted. "It was only three percent interest."

This difference of opinion was not the attendant's problem, and he knew it. It was his supervisor's responsibility to handle such matters. Paul knew all too well what was going on, but for the time being he just stood there on the sideline watching. Nevertheless, he was expecting to be called over any time. And soon enough, he was.

"Mr. Daleddo," the attendant asked politely, "would you come over here please? This lady has a complaint."

Oh, God, he thought. What would he do now? Paul felt so sick and doped up that he could hardly see or think straight. These days the more pressure Paul was put under, the more medicine he was taking, and this had a bad affect on him rather than a good one. Still, he knew that he had an obligation to take care of the problem, so he went over to see what the conflict was.

"May I help you, ma'am?" Paul inquired.

"Yes," she stated belligerently. "This young man says that I owe $4,579 on a loan that I took out last year, when I calculated it to be only $3,925. I don't owe that much interest. I'm sure of it."

"Interest?" he said staring at her. Paul had momentarily forgotten what interest was. He didn't even hear what the woman was saying anymore. He was very close to a fainting spell. The woman was beginning to notice that he seemed incoherent. So was the attendant. Paul stared aimlessly at the floor. He was bending over, leaning his arm against the ledge of the window. By this time everybody in the office realized that Paul was ill. Several of them approached him to see if they could be of any help. But after only a few seconds, when Paul had regained consciousness, he hurried to the nearest men's room. He went in, closed the door, and locked it securely from the inside.

Seeing all the commotion she had caused, the woman naturally felt awkward and embarrassed. "Never mind," she said indignantly. "I'll come back some other time when somebody else is on duty."

For about fifteen minutes, Paul lay flat on the bathroom floor, panting and heaving uncontrollably. He had taken off his jacket and loosened his shirt and tie. Now his whole body was wet. His forehead was shining with perspiration, and his stomach was terribly upset. He was lucky to have a sink and toilet nearby. It was also fortunate that it was air conditioned in that little room. When he finally recovered from his collapse, Paul got up and looked into the mirror above the sink.

At that moment, Paul had to face the reality that he had made a dreadful mistake. He should never have taken on such a responsibility as this in the first place. So why had he taken the job? Paul had to admit it was an offer he thought he could not refuse. He thought it could be an ultimate recovery for him. Deep inside, though, he knew all along that he was neither ready nor competent enough to accept such a demanding position. But Paul still realized that this was a decision he had made and that now he had to deal with it.

Paul turned on the faucet and splashed some cold water over his face. Once he felt sufficiently revived, he adjusted his shirt and tie and picked his jacket up off the floor. After folding it neatly and putting it over his arm, he walked out of the rest room and went back into the main office.

When Paul went back behind the windows, one of the employees asked him an expected question. "Mr. Daleddo," he addressed him. "What happened to you a while ago?"

Paul appeared to be calm and self possessed. "Oh, nothing," he answered. "Just a dizzy spell. That's all."

For the rest of the day, Paul carried on with his work as if nothing at all had happened to him earlier.

The next day Paul went to work as usual. This time he went directly to the main office, where he was supposed to be supervising. At almost exactly the same time, however, the director of the company came down to the office and approached Paul privately.

"Mr. Daleddo," he whispered. "Could you come to my office? I would like to talk to you."

"Yes," Paul replied meekly.

They both went up to the second floor, where the director's office was. The whole time they were climbing the stairs, though, Haller walked in front of Paul and didn't look back at him once. Paul, knowing exactly what this meeting was going to be about, looked down at the stairs. He didn't care to look Haller in the face. When they had both entered the office, Haller walked immediately over to his desk and sat down in his swivel chair.

"Sit down," he said coldly. Once Paul had sat down in front of him, the director began his solemn discourse. "I understand that you had a minor mishap yesterday."

"Yes, I did," Paul confessed.

"Are you feeling better?" he inquired in a formal tone of voice.

"Yes, thank you," Paul answered nervously.

Haller sat back in his chair. "Mr. Daleddo," he said. "You told me that you were a manager at the other company you worked for, didn't you?"

"Yes, I did,"

"Son, I called the Mackenfield Branch in Greensboro this morning. You were not a manager there. You were a subordinate."

When Paul heard this, he could only stare down at the floor. In one sense he felt ashamed—in another, he felt extremely relieved. Living with the horrible lie was putting him under almost unbearable pressure. Yet in another sense, Paul felt good about himself. At least he was making an effort. At least he was trying to better his situation by finding a job. So what if it turned out to be too much for him? He would never have known that if he hadn't made an attempt.

"It's true," Paul nodded. "I was not a manager there."

"I'm sorry," Haller said, "but I'm going to have to let you go. For one thing, we are only looking for people with managerial experience here and for another, even if we weren't, lying is always grounds for termination."

Paul let out a heavy sigh. "I understand." He slowly got up from his chair. At the door he Paul turned back to the director one last time. "Thanks anyway," he told him. Then he walked out.

Chapter 9

It was now late March. The weather was getting warmer in Tunis. The sky was clear, and the sun was shining. There were more people out on the street. This raised Anna's morale and helped her forget recurring problems at work.

Later on that week, Anna saw Noureddine again. She had made arrangements to meet him in one of the cafés in the center of town. After work, Anna went directly to that café. Noureddine had already arrived. He was sitting at one of the small tables near the large front window of the café. Immediately Anna walked over, greeted Noureddine, and sat down opposite him at the table.

Anna noticed that Noureddine had something on his mind. But before she had a chance to ask him what it was, the waiter came over to their table. Once they had both ordered a coffee, Anna folded her hands on the table and bent over close to Noureddine.

"What's up, my dear?" she asked briskly.

After a few moments of thoughtfulness, Noureddine brought up a subject he hadn't talked about in a long time. "Annie," he said. "Do you think that there's any possibility of my living and working in the U.S. once I've finished my studies here in Tunisia?"

Anna looked at him almost apathetically. "Do you really want to?" she challenged him.

"Of course I do," he insisted.

"Noureddine, we've been through this before," Anna lectured him. "You say that you want to go to America, but wait until the time comes, and I'll bet you change your mind."

"Annie, you don't understand," he contradicted her. "That's not the only thing I wanted to ask you today. There's something else that I'd like to talk to you about."

Anna raised her eyebrows curiously. "There is?" she asked.

"Yes, there is," he affirmed. "Annie, what are you doing over spring vacation?"

"Nothing special," she replied casually. "I have no place to go—no friends to travel with. Why do you ask?"

"I was wondering if you wanted to come with me to Gabes, where my parents live. I've told them about you, and they say they would like to meet you. I figured that this spring break would be the perfect time to take you to see them."

Anna was flabbergasted. She had never expected Noureddine to take a bold step like that. But perhaps it was true, she thought. Maybe he really was serious about living and working in the U.S. Anna knew that if Noureddine was willing to introduce her to his family, it was a strong indication that he had future plans for them together.

"Why, of course I'll go with you to meet your family," she said. "I've never seen the south of Tunisia, and I'd like very much to go to Gabes to do some sightseeing."

"Good," Noureddine said. "Spring vacation starts in two weeks. We'll make arrangements."

It was about five in the morning when Anna and Noureddine got ready to leave for Gabes. Instead of taking the bus, they elected to take a louage. A louage was like a car or taxi, only several people rode in it at once. They chose the louage because it was almost exactly the same price as the bus and because it was considerably more comfortable. To Anna, though, this vehicle looked like not much more than an old jalopy. Even so, it was better than an overcrowded bus, where they probably wouldn't have been able to get a seat.

It was about a nine-hour ride to Gabes, which Anna assumed would be lengthy and boring. On the contrary, the trip turned out to be quite fascinating for her. The farther south they traveled, the more the land and people seemed to change.

The first thing Anna noticed as they headed south was that the women seemed to have a different way of dressing. Instead of draping themselves in white veils as they did in Tunis, they wore colorful dresses that were long and loose and tied tightly around their waists with a chain or belt. Some of the women were bare-headed—others wore colored veils knotted around their necks. Even the young girls were dressed in the same manner, rather than wearing modern clothes as they did in Tunis. Though the trip itself was long and tiresome, Anna found all these sub-cultural changes extremely intriguing.

Anna also noted that the farther south they went, the more sparse the vegetation became. While the northern region of Tunisia was green and fertile, the southernmost part was almost barren. By the time they had nearly reached their destination, there was nothing on the ground except for small plants and a tiny bit of grass. No buildings or people could be seen for miles around. At times Anna could hardly believe her eyes, as she had never encountered anything like this before. What she did not realize was that she still had a lot to discover about this area of the country.

Anna knew almost nothing about the culture and customs in the south of Tunisia. She had no idea that it was notably more conservative than the north. Even after all the time Anna had spent in Tunis, she still had not observed that the people there seemed to be closely bound to their traditions but free and liberal. Women went out on the streets whenever they wanted to. The younger girls all went to school, and some even attended college. It seemed as if the young people were free to go out and socialize as they wished, or even to live on their own if they so desired. Unfortunately, Anna had no idea of what went on behind closed doors. She was not aware of what transpired inside the homes of these people, how suppressed the women and children were, the stipulations and restraints that existed within families, and how attached to their honor and values they were.

At last they arrived at Gabes in early afternoon. The weather was even warmer than in Tunis. It was a bright, sunny day. As far as Anna was concerned, the climate and atmosphere of this city struck her fancy right away. It all seemed more authentic and untouched than in Tunis. Horses strolled along pulling carts on the dirt roads of the city. The stores and markets were open, with people on the sidewalks selling their merchandise. Everything from brass pots to bushels of grain could be found here. Anna found this environment quaint, unpretentious, and utterly charming. Little did she know that while this trip would be interesting, at times it would be less than charming.

Noureddine lived some distance from the station, so he needed to call one of his neighbors to pick them up. As soon as the louage pulled into the station, he went inside to telephone one of his friends.

Back with Annie after finishing his phone call, Noureddine said, "I know you. You say and do anything you want to. I think it's better if you keep quiet during this visit. Be very careful about how you act."

Though she had been expecting this lecture all along, Anna was furious. She had discovered a long time ago that Noureddine was extremely conscious of the impression he made on others. Even worse was that he was dumping part of this responsibility on Anna. Any time that they were out with Noureddine's friends in Tunis, he always wanted Anna to put up the front of being the meek, subdued type of woman who was only there to hold the wall up. Anna did not verbally react to what he had just told her. She knew that later on, she and Noureddine would have a few words on the subject.

At last Noureddine's neighbors arrived at the station to pick the two of them up. The car was another run-down vehicle, looking something like the louage Anna and Noureddine had taken down here. Anna understood that having a car, no matter what its shape or condition, was considered a luxury in a country like this.

In the front seat of the car was an older man, with his son sitting next to him in the driver's seat. When they got out, Noureddine greeted them both warmly and introduced them to Anna. Then Anna and Noureddine piled their luggage into the trunk and got into the back seat. Once the other two men were back in the front seat, the boy started up the car again and pulled out of the station.

Almost the entire time that they were riding in the car, the two neighbors were speaking in Arabic to Noureddine. Anna noticed certain peculiarities about both of the gentlemen who were accompanying them to Noureddine's house. The older man had a bloated stomach and bloodshot eyes and smelled strongly of liquor. He also had several stitched-up scars on his face, which looked as if they could have resulted from a violent fight or brawl. The man's son turned Anna off even more. He struck Anna as a mopey, dejected type who had no good will to offer anybody else. Neither of them seemed pleasant to Anna, but she was not offended by them. She recognized right away that it was far beyond their intellectual capacity to extend themselves to an outsider.

After about a half-hour's drive, they arrived at the neighbors' house, which was next door to Noureddine's parents' home. Before being taken to his place, Anna had the pleasure of meeting her chauffeur's mistress, who came outside to meet them as soon as the car pulled up to the house.

She greeted them shyly and then hurried to her boyfriend's side. Judging from her accent and physical appearance, Anna concluded that she was French and not Tunisian. She looked like a good match for Noureddine's neighbor, shallow and stupid in appearance. She felt no need to go out of her way to be friendly. Anna had heard that this girl was down in Gabes living with Noureddine's friend and that neither one of them was working, studying, or married. Anna questioned how his family tolerated such an arrangement, but she realized that this affair was neither her business nor her concern.

At Noureddine's house, when his family saw that he had arrived, they came outside to greet them. Each brother and sister seemed ecstatic to see him, and his parents seemed overjoyed. They were all terribly emotional, and it seemed to Anna that they embraced Noureddine for a full ten minutes. Once they had finally finished greeting their son, Noureddine's parents were introduced to Anna. Only now did Anna began to feel nervous about what she was about to encounter.

"Hello," Noureddine's mother said in Arabic.

"Hi," Anna responded.

Noureddine's mother slowly approached her and kissed her, but Noureddine's father on the other hand, waited for Anna to come to him. So without any more hesitation, she walked over to him and gave him a hug. This seemed to shock the rest of the family, as it was not their custom for a young lady to be so forward on the first meeting. While this reaction didn't seem to bother Anna, she could tell already that Noureddine was getting more and more uptight about this reunion.

Then they all went inside. Noureddine's abode was somewhere between utterly plain and elegant. It was an attractive house with an open courtyard surrounded by rooms on two levels. They entered the living room area and sat down.

At first Anna felt a bit shy and awkward when she found herself surrounded by this strange family. She didn't know what to say or do around a group of people with whom she could hardly communicate. Noureddine started a conversation in Arabic with his family, and Anna felt relieved to be able to sit back and observe what was going on.

On the whole Noureddine's family was attractive. Both of his parents looked to be well over fifty years of age, but his father still seemed healthy and strong, and his mother was impeccably neat and trim for her age. The younger children, looking much like Noureddine and his parents, were all docile. They sat quietly on the sofa while Noureddine talked to his parents. The children watched Anna, noticing the small ways that she was different from them. This no longer disturbed Anna. She was getting used to this new atmosphere, and understood the children's curiosity.

Noureddine was the oldest boy in the family. He had only one older sister. He was also a child of polygamy. His father once had three wives. Today, however, polygamous matrimonies no longer existed in Tunisia. When the president of the Republic came into power after Tunisia acquired its independence, he outlawed these marriages once and for all. But fortunately, Noureddine's father had married his third wife just before this declaration was made. From his three marriages, his father had eleven children. One wife was no longer living with them. Noureddine had explained to Anna that the second spouse did not like the idea of sharing her husband with anybody else. So now the only women living with Noureddine's father were his other two wives. Noureddine had also explained to Anna that the youngest spouse lived on the upper level with her children, while Noureddine's mother, brothers, and sisters lived on the ground floor. Anna often wondered how this arrangement worked out, but she didn't dare to ask Noureddine about it.

Soon after they had arrived at the house, Noureddine's mother prepared some tea for all of them. She brought it into the living room and set it down on a small table so that all could serve themselves. Noureddine's parents then started a conversation in Arabic with their son about her.

"Where did you meet this girl?" Noureddine's mother inquired.

"I met her in Tunis," he answered nervously. "I had some business to take care of at the Institute where she was working, and she was one of the people I conferred with over there."

"You had some business to take care of?" his father asked suspiciously. "What kind of business?"

"Academic business," Noureddine blurted. "I needed to know something about the United States for one of my courses, and she provided me with the information."

"Oh," his mother sighed. "But what did you say that she did for a living?"

"She's a teacher," Noureddine boasted. "As a matter of fact, her official title at the Institute is 'associate professor.'"

"Oh, my," Noureddine's father remarked. "She seems awfully young to be taking on such a responsibility."

"Really, she's quite competent," Noureddine said. "I get the impression that she loves her job and that she's one of the best teachers in her department."

It was a good thing Anna did not understand what was being said. What kind of idol was Noureddine trying to make her out to be? She must have come off as being nothing less than perfect. Little did Noureddine know that he was making a grave mistake. What he did not take into account was that, if Anna and Noureddine ever did get together, his family would be disappointed to find out that Anna was not flawless.

"But isn't she afraid to be here all alone?" his mother questioned. "Don't her parents worry about her?"

"That I don't know," Noureddine confessed. "I never asked her about it. All I can say is that she must have had a lot of guts to come here the way she did."

This was probably the most honest statement he had made about Anna since they got there. It was true. Anna did have nerves of steel. All Anna wanted was for Noureddine's parents to have a realistic image of her—one that was neither overly flattering nor terribly degrading. However, Anna didn't care much what Noureddine was saying about her to his parents. She figured that sooner or later it would be up to her to portray an appropriate image of herself.

When the tea and conversation were finished, Anna and Noureddine just relaxed, watched television, and ate dinner in the evening. When it was time to go to bed, Anna was escorted to her room and Noureddine to his. Anna preferred it that way. She felt that what she did with Noureddine when they were on their own was their business, but when they were in his parents' home, a certain protocol should be followed. For that matter, if she had been in her own parents' home, Anna would have done the same thing. So that night Anna slept alone, undisturbed and with a clear conscience.

The next morning, Noureddine told Anna that they were going to his neighbors' house for lunch. They were supposed to be there at noon. Then Noureddine started once again with his "behavior" lecture.

"Just keep quiet," he told her. "Don't say or do anything to offend anybody."

"Don't worry, Noureddine," Anna said. "I'll do what I think is right. I won't have you telling me how to act all the time."

"Just be careful," Noureddine insisted. "I don't want you to make a bad impression that's all."

"I'm not going to make a bad impression. Besides, if I do make a bad impression, it's the only kind of impression I can make. Right? Right!"

"I get the message, Annie," Noureddine said. "You know darn well how to act, and you're only saying that to provoke me."

"You never know," Anna said slyly. "I might make a bad impression on purpose."

"Don't you dare."

"Noureddine, the only way you can keep me from messing it up while I'm here is to LAY OFF. That's all I want."

"All right. I'll lay off if you'll be careful, and I won't say anything more about it."

Anna realized that Noureddine had gotten the message. What she did not realize, though, was that she still had not heard the end of this issue. It was true that Noureddine would not say anything more about it, but he would definitely do something.

When they got to the neighbors' house, the man's son, whose name was Ali, answered the door. His girlfriend was standing right beside him. Neither of them seemed to be in a good mood.

"Hi," Ali grunted. He gestured for them to come in.

His girlfriend didn't say anything as they entered the house. When Anna saw what she was about to encounter, she shrugged inside. Oh, brother, she thought. She honestly didn't understand why she had to be so careful around such imbeciles as these neighbors.

At any rate, they soon went into the dining room, where the table was set for lunch. The table was quite big, so Anna assumed that the whole family would be there that day. Soon enough, everybody came into the dining room and sat down. This included both of Ali's parents and all of his brothers and sisters.

This good Moslem family started out by serving everybody some wine. The wife and younger children, however, did not partake of it. But for everybody else, Ali's father seemed to want to push it. As soon as he had swilled down his first glass of wine, he eagerly poured himself another, took a quick gulp, and set it down in front of his plate.

"You know," he sighed. "When I drink this wine, I think of the time when Tunisia was still a French colony."

"Oh, really?" Anna responded. "How's that?"

"Tunisia was a good place when France had possession of it," he said, "but it's an even better place now."

"Oh," Anna said. "That makes sense." At that moment Anna felt a nudge from Noureddine, who was sitting beside her.

"You know something else?" the man continued. "I can't get over how we lambasted the French during the revolution."

"Oh, really?" Anna repeated. "How long ago was that?"

Then the man got a little fidgity. "I don't remember," he said, embarrassed. "It was some time ago, though."

Anna did not respond to that last bit of information. It was obvious to her that this gentleman was less than a history buff. She figured it would be better to drop the whole subject. But to her dismay, it seemed that the old man didn't want it that way.

"But there's one thing that I do remember about that war," he added.

"What's that?" Anna humored him.

"I remember that we knocked them dead. The French had no choice but to give us our independence."

"Then you must have served in that war," Anna said. "You seem to know quite a bit about it." At that moment Anna felt another, more penetrating nudge from Noureddine.

"No," the man confessed. "As a matter of fact, I didn't. But I had so many buddies that served that I've become pretty well versed on the topic."

"Oh." Anna thought that it was high time to change the subject. "This lunch is very good. What type of grain did you say this was?"

"It's couscous," the girlfriend answered.

"Couscous," Anna repeated. "I noticed that they eat a lot of that in France." For some strange reason, Noureddine gave Anna an even more pronounced pinch on the hip. With that Anna turned toward him and gave him a cold stare. "Why are you doing that?" she asked him under her breath.

"Can't you take a joke?" he kidded her. Then he turned their attention toward the other people at the table.

Later on that day, when they returned to Noureddine's house, he was the first to bring up the disagreement that he'd had with Anna. "Annie," he said, "Were you startled when I nudged you that last time?"

"No, I was more like disgusted," Anna said, "because I was sure you weren't doing it just to play around."

"Oh, really? Then why was I doing it?"

"You were trying to tell me something, and you know it."

"I didn't mean anything nasty by it," Noureddine retorted. "I only wanted you to be on guard. That's all."

"On guard? On guard about what? What did I do today to disturb you or anybody else at your neighbors' house?"

"Nothing. I just didn't want you to say too much."

That feeble response was the last straw, but instead of flaring up at him, Anna decided to do something more effective. She elected to bow out of the whole argument completely. "Noureddine," she said, "I have a solution for both of us. If you find me incapable of making a good impression when we go out somewhere with your friends, I won't go anymore. It's as simple as that."

"Annie," Noureddine said. "That's not what I had in mind."

"Why shouldn't it be?" Anna questioned him. "If it's such a hassle for both of us be 'on guard,' then we won't go

anywhere where we have to worry about being 'on guard.'"
Her tone was biting and sarcastic.

"Annie," Noureddine repeated. "That's not what I
wanted, and you know it."

"Maybe it's what I want. After all, I'm entitled to my
own preferences, too."

Noureddine was getting a little aggravated by Anna's
stubbornness. "All right," he grumbled. "Have it your way."

"Good," Anna confirmed. "So the next time you're
afraid that I'll 'say too much,' you might just as well leave
me at home."

Anna was sure that Noureddine had gotten the message. She was strong, and Noureddine knew it. He knew
that she could go out and make it on her own any time that
she cared to. But perhaps that was the most questionable
characteristic of their relationship. Why did Anna stay with
such a chauvinistic man if she considered herself to be so
independent? Because she loved him, of course. But why
did she love him? Perhaps it was because they were such an
appropriate contrast to each other.

At times Anna acted as if she didn't care enough what
people thought of her, and at other times Noureddine acted
as if he cared too much. Yet there was more to it than this.
Whatever his faults, Anna knew that Noureddine was a serious person. If nothing else, the type of behavior that Ali and
his girlfriend displayed was a good basis for comparison.
Anna was aware that Noureddine was not like Ali, so it
would be only natural that he didn't expect Anna to be like
Ali's girlfriend. As much as she resented the one side of
their disagreement, she greatly appreciated its other aspect.
If Noureddine had high standards for Anna, it meant that he
thought more of her than he would have somebody else.
Anna realized that if Noureddine didn't care about her, he
wouldn't care about what others thought of her as well. He
also would not take any of her rebuttals. Anna was sure that

Noureddine loved her very much, and that was all she needed to know.

Throughout the vacation, Anna was received well by all of Noureddine's relatives. This acceptance amazed her, as she had heard that most Arabic families were clannish by nature. On the contrary, Anna found the people at the house to be hospitable to her during her entire stay.

One reality, however, Anna did not recognize at that time. An ugly scene awaited her, and Anna had no inkling about how the event would come to pass. The reason for the scandal that would later take place was the decision of Noureddine's younger sister, Monia, to go out on her own one day. Though this choice did not seem to be a crucial matter, the situation was complicated by the fact that Monia had made arrangements to meet a male comrade even though she knew she was forbidden to do so.

Earlier that day Monia approached her brother in strictest confidence about her plans to meet her friend in the city.

"Noureddine," she said quietly. "Don't tell Papa, but I'm going to the marketplace to see Mohammed today. He'll be waiting for me there."

"As you wish," Noureddine replied, not taking a position on her decision because if Monia were to get caught by her father, he would rather have it be her responsibility and not his.

Unluckily for Monia, it happened that Noureddine's father was headed to the exact same place where his daughter and her gentleman friend were going—the marketplace in the center of the city. Though the two of them did not leave the house at the same time, their paths there in town would inevitably coincide.

It was high noon, and many people were out doing their daily shopping when Noureddine's father spotted the two of them together in the street. There he stood, tall and rigid, peering through the crowd at his daughter walking alongside her friend. Her father's expression turned frightfully stern and his lips grew tight, but he did nothing to attract their attention. Instead, he threw his cloak over his shoulder and kept on walking up the street, as Monia and her friend continued walking the opposite direction.

Later that afternoon, her father went home and found Anna and Noureddine in the living room reading. Both of them seemed unaware of what Monia might be doing. Still severe and unemotional, Noureddine's father took off his cloak and hung it on a nearby coat rack in the corner of the room. He then walked into the kitchen, and opened one of the upper cupboards. On one of the lower shelves was a heavy leather strap (the kind they use to make horses move when they don't want to budge on their own).

He took the strap out of the cupboard and put it under the faucet of the sink, where he wet it entirely. Then he took the soaked piece of leather and folded it up in his hand so that nobody could see it. He went into the living room and sat down on the sofa. There he waited, acting as calm and undisturbed as Anna and Noureddine.

About half an hour later, his daughter arrived. She walked into the room nonchalantly. The minute she entered the room her father got up and grabbed his daughter's arm with one hand, and with the other, he began whipping the her ruthlessly. Once he started beating his daughter, he did not stop when there were welts and bruises all over her body. He did not stop when her hair was falling out in strands. He did not stop until blood ran from the girl's mouth and nose.

When at last he did stop, he took his daughter, and with one forceful thrust he threw her toward the lower part of the sofa. He hurled her so hard that she knocked her head against the framework of the couch. She knelt on the floor, curled up against one leg of the sofa, in such pain and agony that she could hardly move.

When she heard her daughter's frightening screams, Noureddine's mother rushed into the living room to learn what was going on. The moment she saw Monia crouched against the sofa and her husband standing there with the strap in his hand, she understood immediately what had happened. Her husband scowled at her in a most contemptuous manner.

"If you say or do anything to try and defend Monia, I'll throw you both out of this house!" he shouted.

Inside, Noureddine's mother was crying and suffering as much as her daughter was. She wanted desperately to go over and heal all of Monia's physical and emotional scars, but she didn't dare in her husband's presence. Even so, Noureddine's mother was so hurt, so upset, so overwrought, that she left the room.

Noureddine did not tense up once during the whole time he watched his sister being beaten brutally. Though he realized the seriousness of his father's actions, he just sat on the sofa and observed what was going on. But also there to witness what had happened was Anna, who could not believe her eyes. Oh, my God! she said silently. An American father could be put in jail for something like this. Not only was she appalled by what this man had done to his own daughter, she was equally shocked by his son's indifference.

That night the whole family was quiet and withdrawn. Nobody ate much at dinner time. Monia was not present at the meal. Once everybody had finished eating, Anna got up and went to her bedroom. Staying there alone, however, she found that she could not stop thinking about what happened. She simply had to go and talk to Noureddine about it.

Anna found Noureddine standing near the window, looking outside and finishing a cigarette. The room was almost dark. When he heard Anna come in, he slowly turned to see who was there. He said nothing, but turned and continued staring out the window.

Anna came close to Noureddine and dared to ask him the most obvious question she had on her mind. "Noureddine," she said quietly. "Why did he do it?"

Noureddine let out a heavy sigh, since he was anticipating Anna's interrogation. "It's his conception of discipline and punishment," he replied, still looking out the window.

"Is that all you have to say?" Anna challenged him. "Do you think that what he did was right?"

"I'm in no position to make a judgment," Noureddine said. "I only know that he did what he did. That's all."

Now Anna astonished by what she was hearing. "Noureddine," she said, "in my country what your father did would be considered child abuse."

"We're not in your country, Annie."

Anna was in disbelief of what Noureddine was saying to her and worried sick. She knew that if Noureddine did go along with his father's actions, it meant that he might do the same thing someday. She knew that "someday" might come all too soon for Anna.

"Noureddine," she said. "I don't know how you perceive that kind of behavior, but I hope you know that I would not tolerate it for a minute. I want you to understand that."

"Don't worry about it, Annie," Noureddine said. "Just because my sister and mother took it doesn't mean that you have to."

Anna did not respond. After such a stressful episode, she figured it would be better to leave the whole matter alone. After Noureddine threw the cigarette butt on the floor, he put both of his hands on Anna's shoulders and moved her in front of him near the window. He crossed his arms over the upper part of her chest as she leaned her back against his body. Then they both stared out the window. They said nothing more.

Chapter 10

Before she knew it, Anna was back in Tunis. Her job was going as badly as ever. Not only did she have poor discipline in her classes, she also found it almost impossible to keep her distance from the students inside or outside the Institute. Needless to say, this affected her ability to discipline them.

Every time she threatened to get tougher on a student, he would change his tone and beg for forgiveness. Anna was caught in a vicious circle of people who loved her as a human being but had absolutely no respect for her as an authority. She believed that nothing worse could possibly transpire than what had already happened to her. Much to her dismay, however, Anna would soon find that something much worse would happen concerning her job.

One morning when Anna went to work, she arrived a little later than usual. When she opened the door to her first class, the room was empty. There was absolutely nothing in the classroom but tables and chairs. When Anna took a quick look at her watch, she noted that it was already 8:07 a.m.

More often than not, by this time most of her students were in the classroom, screaming and yelling, hanging out of the windows and knocking over the desks and chairs. So why was no one there today? she wondered.

Only about two minutes after Anna had sat down at her desk in the front of the classroom, one of the students came in, picked up one of the chairs, and carried it out of the room. The girl was smiling ear to ear as she walked out. Less than a minute later two other students, a boy and a girl, came into the room and did the same thing. They, too, were smirking. Then the whole class, one by one, came into the room, took every chair, and carried them out of the class.

Anna turned around at her desk and looked through the partially opened door of the classroom to find out what was going on. All of the students had made a large circle with the chairs out in the hallway.

Anna didn't dare try to figure out on her own what they were trying to prove by doing this, so she got up from her desk and walked over to the classroom door to have a word with them. "Are you coming to class or not?" she asked.

"No, we're not coming to class," said one of the students. "If you want us to come to your class, call Mr. Ben Hassen."

"You call Mr. Ben Hassen," Anna replied. "You have three minutes to get into this class. After that, you'll all be considered to be cutting." She then closed the classroom door and went back to her desk.

About ten minutes passed. Then the door opened quietly. Anna now saw the head administrator, Mr. Mustapha Ben Hassen, standing in the doorway. Ben Hassen noticed right away that Anna was still sitting at her desk, writing down the name of each student from the class on her absentee sheet.

Ben Hassen motioned for all the students to come into the class, and they moved everything back into the room, making quite a bit of noise and commotion in so doing. Then Ben Hassen took a chair in front of the room and sat down next to Anna.

"Mademoiselle," Ben Hassen addressed her in French. "Would you excuse me, please? I am going to speak to them in Arabic."

"Yes," Anna consented. "Go ahead."

Soon everybody in the classroom began conversing with Ben Hassen in a language she did not understand whatsoever. She did, however, manage to pick up certain words out of their French-ified dialect of Arabic. Anna heard such terms as "comprehension" and "composition" in a language she was familiar with.

She even caught something about one of the students from that class going in and spying on one of her other classes that taught a different subject matter. The more she heard them talk, the more certain Anna was becoming that the entire class was in the process of downgrading her as a teacher to her supervisor. Something about the way they were speaking to Ben Hassen made her sure that it was true. Anna did not yet know half the story.

Once Ben Hassen had completed a somewhat lengthy discussion with the students, he got up from his seat and turned toward Anna. "Mademoiselle," he addressed her again. "Please continue your course as you normally would." Then he left the room.

"What was that all about?" Anna questioned her students.

"It was about you," one of the students said.

"About me?" Anna repeated.

"Yes," replied another student. "We told Mr. Ben Hassen that you weren't teaching us anything."

"Oh," Anna responded sharply. "Is that so?"

"Yes," repeated the first student. "We were comparing your class with other courses we are taking. We said that your course is far inferior to our other classes."

As much as Anna had misfired throughout the entire school year, she knew better than to argue with the class. She recognized immediately that what these students had done was so sick and sadistic that it did not even merit discussion. So instead, Anna simply elected to take a completely different approach.

"Very well," she said. "If you are not learning anything in my class, maybe it would be better if we ended it for the time being. After all, I don't want to waste anybody's time." Without another moment to lose, Anna picked up all of her things from her desk and walked to the door. "Once you've figured out that sitting around in cafés all day isn't going to prepare you any more for your test than I will, you can come back." Then she walked out.

Once she had finished her classes that day, Anna knew she would have to go to see Ben Hassen about what had transpired that morning. She was not at all looking forward to it, but she knew that if she didn't go to him, he would soon come to her. So right away she walked down to his office, opened the door, and went inside. When Ben Hassen saw that she was there, he greeted her in a surprisingly cordial manner.

"Please sit down," he invited her, pointing to one of the chairs in front of his desk.

"What was going on during that class this morning?" she asked as she sat down.

"The students told me that they weren't learning anything from your course," he informed her. "They also said that they did not consider you a real teacher."

A real teacher? Anna thought. What the hell was that supposed to mean? But before she even had a chance to ponder it, one of Anna's other supervisors entered the office. This time it was Dr. Brahim Santani, the head of the English department. Of all the authorities Anna had above her, Brahim was the one Anna esteemed the most. As far as she was concerned, he was the one who really knew what he was doing. He was the only one who was self assured. He was the only one detached enough to be respected, yet personable enough to be loved. To Anna, Dr. Santani was the only one who was a real professional.

As soon as he entered the room, Brahim sat down next to Anna. "What happened, Annie?" he questioned her.

"It's that same class that has been giving me trouble since the beginning of the year," Anna said. "I can't believe what they've done."

Brahim and Ben Hassen decided to speak to each other in Arabic. After a few brief moments of discussion, Brahim seemed to understand rather well what had occurred earlier that day. He did, in fact, know more about what the students had said to Ben Hassen than Anna did.

"Annie," Brahim said in English. "You shouldn't talk about your private life to your students. This gives them an excuse to misbehave and criticize the teacher later on. They all like to have something to joke about, but afterward, it is always difficult to get control of the class again."

Now Anna was catching on pretty fast as to what her class was telling their administrator that morning. "Brahim," she responded. "They are the ones who have encouraged that kind of conversation since the beginning of the year. They're always asking me personal questions."

"But don't you know that they're setting you up for trouble?" Brahim said. "They're doing it to establish a close relationship with you, and later they will use this to exploit you."

Anna felt ashamed. How true it was, she admitted. She had given her students a good reason to misbehave, and now they were using it against her.

It was pointless for Anna to reflect now on what she should have done at the beginning of the year to correct the problem. Things were too far gone to think about that. But one thing, Anna still did not understand. In a country where oppression and discipline seemed to prevail, she wondered how the students could do such a thing and get away with it. Surely there must have been more order in the school system than that. Anna would soon find, however, that nothing could be farther from the truth.

"Brahim," she addressed her supervisor. "I honestly can't get over the idea that those students would do something like that. Where on earth did they ever get it in their heads to pull such a prank?"

When he heard this, Brahim acted somewhat embarrassed. "Annie," he clarified. "That was nothing by comparison to what they did last year. Almost all the freshmen and sophomores last year failed because they refused to take their final exams."

"Why did they all refuse to take their exams? Didn't they know that they would fail?"

Ben Hassen understood enough English to get the general idea of what the two of them were talking about. "They most certainly did," he added in French. "But they all went along with it because it was a group effort to tell us something."

"Tell you something? Tell you what?"

The two men hesitated. "They were trying to tell us something about the whole system we have here," Brahim said. "They feel they aren't getting enough representation."

"Oh," Anna recalled. "Come to think of it, I heard something about that strike. Wasn't it about the same time as that mass demonstration that took place here in Tunis?"

Her two supervisors shuddered. Anna had just stepped into forbidden territory. The event Anna had mentioned was one that indicated a serious turnaround in the political attitudes of the Tunisian people. It was also the first sign of a serious threat to their government. Anna had just implied that the reaction of the students toward the Institute had something to do with the Tunisian people's reaction to the government. To her it made a lot of sense. It was exactly this that was the problem.

"Yes," Ben Hassen verified. "It was at about the same time."

Then Brahim quickly changed the subject. "Annie," he said calmly. "I hope you understand how important it is to remain tough with those students. If not, they'll walk all over you."

Anna forced a dull laugh. "You know," she sighed. "It's strange. The whole time I was teaching here, I thought that it would be just the opposite. I thought that if I got tough with the students, they would start rebelling. It looks as if suppression is the only thing they understand."

Now Brahim acted even more embarrassed. "Yes," he humbly agreed. "Unfortunately, that's true."

Anna saw no point in continuing the discussion, so she got ready to leave the office. "Thank you very much for seeing me today," she told them both. "I will do my best to improve the situation." Then she went over to the office door, opened it, and walked out.

As Anna was walking down the stairs, she thought about it. Brahim and Ben Hassen were quite supportive of her, considering the circumstances. That was really decent of them. If it had been the director, Anna knew that he would have never let her hear the end of it. Little did Anna know at this time that, thanks to the director, she had by no means heard the end of it.

The next day Anna went to that same class. They seemed more subdued than normal, but this did not surprise her. She figured that they wanted to stay on the good side of the administrators and that by displaying good behavior, that would be easier to do. As she began her class, she did so as she normally would have. She began reading an excerpt in English, which the students would try to interpret. She wasn't halfway into the reading, however, when a knock was heard on her classroom door. As soon as she walked to the door and opened it, Anna saw that it was nobody less than the director himself. It was no mystery for Anna to guess why he was standing there.

"Miss Daleddo," he said in his usual formal tone of voice. "Is this the class that is creating problems?"

"Yes," Anna nodded reluctantly. "This is the one."

"Could you give me a few moments alone with these students? I would like to talk to them about this matter."

Oh, brother, Anna thought. Now her goose was really cooked. She knew that the director would have absolutely no respect for what she might have to say once the students were through with her. Still, what choice did she have? The director was her boss, and the students wanted to have their say. So she consented.

"All right," she said. "I'll wait outside."

As the director closed the door, Anna sat on one of the chairs out in the hall. She soon heard talking and heckling coming from inside the classroom. Anna didn't dare try to guess what they all were saying about her. She knew it would be too painful for her to hear. As it turned out, the director was in that classroom for more than twenty minutes before he finally opened the door and came out. He seemed surprisingly uptight and nervous as he approached Anna.

"I would like to see you as soon as possible," he told her. "I believe the problem to be one of an administrative nature."

An administrative nature? Anna thought. What kind of "mumbo jumbo" was that? Anna reckoned that this was probably the director's way of sweeping the whole issue under the rug. So he wanted to see her as soon as possible, Anna thought. She would make sure that such a time was as far away as possible.

Anna didn't go to see the director. She supposed that if he had anything else to say to her, it would be easy enough for him to come to her as he had before. The same went for the students. There was nothing they could do to her now, that they hadn't already tried before. But one dilemma remained in Anna's mind—the question of job security.

Anna realized that her position at the Institute was in serious jeopardy. She knew deep inside that a strong possibility existed that she would not be there much longer. While reading the contract several times before signing it, she had noted the last clause, which stated that any employee could be terminated at any time in a case where professional incompetence was evident. At this stage of the game, displaying professional incompetence would be an understatement in how her superiors described her job performance.

The more she thought about it, the more it worried her. What would Anna do if she lost her job? How would she find another? Where would she go to live? The questions in her mind became overwhelming.

Then she thought about somebody else in much greater distress than she was in—her brother. All of a sudden she saw a parallel between the destinies of herself and her sibling. That afternoon she went back to her apartment, got herself a pen and paper and started writing a letter to Paul. It read as follows:

Dear Paul,

I really don't know how to begin this letter, so I'll start by saying that I hope you're doing better these days. As for me, things aren't going very well at all.

I mentioned before that I was having discipline problems at work, but that isn't the half of what's going on now. Last week a group of my students got together and said every downgrading thing about me that they possibly could think of to the main administrator here at the Institute. The way it seems to me, my students sound a lot like that "Danny" guy you were working with when you were at Steamers.

They're all a bunch of sick cases, I'm telling you. Honestly, Paul, I don't know about this job any more. If things don't start looking up damn soon, I may not last the two years that I'm supposed to. That, I truly believe.

So don't feel so bad about your situation, dear brother. Things couldn't be going much worse for you than they are for me right now. Take care of yourself.

Your loving sister,
Annie

As soon as she finished the letter, Anna put it in an envelope, addressed it, and put a stamp on it. She went downstairs and mailed it. Then she put it out of her mind.

That night Anna was having Noureddine over to dinner. She was not a half-bad cook, as shown by her previous endeavors. She was, however, somewhat unorthodox. She rarely measured ingredients before she put them into a mixture and almost never followed a recipe. Nonetheless, her results were usually tasty, creative, and unique. So there she was, in her small kitchen with an apron on, sauteing some prime beef in her own special way.

As she shuffled meat around in the pan with her fork, Anna was also frying some onions. After throwing some spices into the pan, she picked up some of the onions with her fork, blew them lightly to cool them, and tasted them. Then she put the fork back into the frying pan in order to turn the meat again. Delicious, she thought. Noureddine will be so happy with this dinner. The doorbell rang. Anna went into the hallway to answer it. Noureddine was standing there, holding a bottle of wine in his hand.

"Hi," she said with a smile. "Glad you could make it."

After she let Noureddine in, he handed her the wine, and they went back into the kitchen together. Noureddine, looked at what was in the frying pan. "That looks very good," he commented. "And I'm starving."

"Good," Anna replied as she set the wine on the kitchen table. "It'll be ready soon."

Anna picked up the fork to turn the meat again, but before she could do so, she dropped it on the floor. After bending to pick it up, she proceeded to use the fork as she was going to before. When he saw this, Noureddine grabbed her hand.

"Don't do that, Annie," he advised her. "That fork is dirty. Go get a clean one."

"It doesn't matter," Anna argued. "It's just a fork. And besides, my floor is clean."

Noureddine's voice got a firmer. "Get another fork, I said," he ordered her. "Do not put that one back in the pan." Then he grabbed the fork out of her hand.

Anna seemed to be getting obstinate for its own sake. "Give me back my fork," she demanded. "Who's making this dinner, anyway?" Anna tried to get the fork back from him, but Noureddine put it behind his back with one hand and with the other, fought Anna off. After a few seconds, Anna, not having much of a sense of humor tonight, recognized that this charade was ridiculous. She reached over to the stove, turned off the gas burner under the cooking meat, and stormed into her bedroom. "Make the dinner yourself," she called back to Noureddine.

Noureddine, realizing that this argument had gotten quite silly, went into the bedroom. There he found Anna, lying on the bed with her head in a pillow. He sat down next to her and patted her lightly on the back. "I'm sorry, Annie," he apologized. "It's just that some of your habits bother me."

My habits? This made Anna boil inside. Noureddine was not exactly a model of perfection himself. What right did he have to criticize her for a little thing like a fork that slipped to the floor? She sobbed some more.

After a while she raised her head from the pillow and reached over to get a tissue from a box on her night table. "I'm sorry, too," she said, blowing her nose. "But it's not about the meal that I'm sorry. It's about other things."

"Oh, really? Like what?"

"It's the same old thing," Anna moaned. "It's my job. They are determined to make my life a living hell."

Noureddine had heard all this before. Still, he tried to be supportive. "Annie, what are you so uptight about?" he rationalized. "You have a contract, and that's binding. They couldn't terminate you even if they wanted to."

"Oh, yes they can," Anna contradicted him. "I was just thinking about it today. The last clause of my contract says something about being able to get rid of somebody who is 'professionally incompetent.' " Anna changed her tone of voice saying those last two words.

Noureddine took a deep breath and shrugged his shoulders. "Wait till the end of the year and see what happens. I suppose you will know something by then." He still didn't seem terribly concerned.

Sure. See what happens. To Anna that was like putting her head on the chopping block and just waiting to "see what happens." In a way, though, she knew that Noureddine was right. Worrying and anticipating the worst was doing Anna absolutely no good. If anything, it was making her more paranoid every time she entered the Institute. So Anna forced herself to forget about it, at least for the time being. Soon she got up from her bed and blew her nose one more time.

"Noureddine," she said as she looked up at him. "Let's finish making dinner."

Chapter 11

Ever since the incident with National Exchange, Inc., Paul had little motivation to do much of anything. His once vivid dream of getting back on top of things was shattered, and he had no idea how to get his life back on track. The problem was that he was slowly but surely running out of money and would soon have to take just about any job he could find.

A couple of days earlier, a friend of Paul's had told him about an opening for a security position at a nearby office building. An easy enough job, Paul concluded. All he'd really have to do would be to stand guard at the door and monitor all the people who came and went. So that morning, he got on the phone as he had before and called the company to whom he had been referred.

Paul went in for a brief interview that afternoon, and they told him that he would suit the position just fine. So they issued Paul a uniform and ID card and sent him on his way, instructing him to be there promptly the next morning. Paul had to admit that he was not nearly as enthusiastic about this job as he had been about his last position. It was indeed a step down, and his pay would be a fraction of what he was used to getting. But what choice did he have? He would have to start earning a living again sooner or later. Besides, Paul really did need something to do.

The following morning Paul rose bright and early. Though still groggy, he was determined to make a go of it that day. So he staggered into the kitchen, still half asleep, to find Louise already sitting at the table having a cup of coffee. He pulled out the chair across from her and almost fell into it.

"Paul," Louise raised her eyebrows. "Are you all right?"

"Not really," Paul mumbled. "I'm still pretty tired."

"Let me pour you some coffee," Louise suggested. "It'll help perk you up."

"OK," Paul said, nodding listlessly. "Whatever you say."

Louise pulled a cup and saucer from the cupboard. She set them on the counter next to the coffee maker, picked up the pot by the handle and poured Paul a steaming cup. Then she went over to the table and set the cup and saucer in front of him.

"Here," she said. "That ought to do the trick."

"Sure," Paul said.

Then he picked up the cup and took a sip of coffee. Slowly, he drank the entire cup, and actually did feel revived. He felt so good, in fact, that he decided to have some more. So he went up to the coffee maker, poured himself another cup, and sat back down. After he had finished his second cup, Paul could honestly say that he was wide awake. He then got up from the table and went to his room to get dressed for work.

Within less than two hours Paul was at his new job, sitting at a desk right by the entrance of a huge office building. He was still in a good mood, which he attributed to all that miraculous coffee he drank that morning. As there were not too many people coming and going at the time, Paul decided to give his mother a call to thank her for her sound advice. When the phone rang in Louise's bedroom, she went over and picked it up.

"Hello?" she responded.

"Hi, this is Paul."

Louise was a little worried to discover that Paul was calling so soon. "Oh, hi, Paul." she greeted him as she sat on the bed. "Is something wrong?"

"Oh, no, not at all. I just wanted to tell you that it was a great idea you had. That coffee really made me feel great."

"Oh," Louise smiled with relief. "Well, I told you that it would perk you up."

"You were right." Then suddenly Paul spotted two people coming into the building. "Listen," he said enthusiastically. "I've got to go. I just wanted to thank you."

"OK," Louise said. "I guess I'll see you this evening."

"Sure thing." Paul hung up.

Strange, Louise thought, how one or two cups of coffee could make such a difference in somebody's outlook. Oh, well. Her son must know what he was talking about.

About four o'clock in the afternoon, Louise was sitting alone in the kitchen when she heard the back screen door open. Who could that be? Paul wasn't due to get off until about 6 p.m. As Louise turned toward the door, she saw that it was indeed her son.

He walked into the kitchen listlessly, pulled out a chair at the kitchen table, and plopped down into it. Louise displayed a confused expression.

"Paul," she said. "Aren't you home a little early?"

Paul did not even look up at his mother. "I quit," he said. "I'm not going back to that job."

"Why?" Louise asked, shaking her head in astonishment. "You just started. Besides, I thought you were happy there."

"I just quit," Paul repeated, still looking down at the table. "I don't want to work there any more."

Louise knew that there was no point in trying to get any kind of rational explanation out of a person who didn't make much sense. She let out a discouraged sigh and walked out of the kitchen.

Ever since his nervous breakdown, Paul did not have much of a social life. He still had a few friends but preferred to keep his distance from them. The reason was not that he thought any less of them, but more because of himself. Paul was embarrassed about his present condition and afraid that if he got too close to his old comrades, the truth about his illness would become evident. (Most of Paul's friends knew that he had left his job in North Carolina but were not aware that he'd had a total breakdown.) So these days Paul spent most of his time by himself, either in his home or by going out on his own.

Then one day Paul was invited to the wedding of one of his friends. He felt that he could not turn it down, because not only was this a long-standing companion of his, but Paul also knew his friends fiancee fairly well. So the day he received the invitation, Paul decided to go.

The afternoon that the wedding was to take place, Paul looked polished and dapper. He was wearing one of his best suits, complemented with a color-coordinated shirt and tie. Even Paul's parents were impressed by what looked to them to be their old son back, stylish and handsome. Paul himself felt his mood elevate as he looked at himself in the mirror one last time before he left the house. He was proud to see a reflection of the person he had thought would never return. At any rate, when Paul was ready to go, he picked up the wedding present that he had bought for the couple, got in his car, and took off.

The ceremony took place in a church with the couple exchanging their vows, kissing, and then departing into what appeared to be a new life. It didn't seem to affect Paul one way or the other, since the ceremony seemed so typical. Once he arrived at the reception, however, some romantic music and a few drinks soon altered his disposition.

It was the normal type of festivity with food, an open bar, and dancing. When Paul saw everybody having such a good time, it began to bother him. The more lightly everybody seemed to be taking the occasion, the more seriously Paul felt about it. The event brought up something crucial in his own life—his future. Would he ever get married? And what about sex? He had always had a problem with that.

As the night lingered, Paul had already had several mixed drinks. With a live band playing and many people dancing, Paul had several opportunities to participate, but he didn't. He just sat and watched the people enjoy themselves.

Paul could not help but observe several young couples who were on the floor. He noticed that they were behaving in an uninhibited manner. Not only were they kissing the whole time they were dancing, but Paul could see their hands wandering. Paul was disgusted by this—but in another way, he was envious. Deep inside, Paul knew that he never had it in him to let himself go enough to do something like that with a girl, and an even bigger concern was that he didn't know if he ever would. So much for his future with women.

Paul had a mediocre time at the wedding, but he did manage to stay for the whole reception. When the celebration ended, Paul left the hall feeling intoxicated and disoriented. He drove home as quickly as possible.

When he arrived, Paul found both of his parents sitting outside, since it was a warm, humid evening. When he saw Paul come around the back of the house, his father greeted him.

"Hi, Paul." he called out as his son walked over to them. "How was the wedding?"

"OK," Paul replied in a muffled voice. Paul took off his jacket and tossed it onto a nearby chair. Then he sat down in one of the chairs beside his parents and loosened his shirt and tie.

Louise noticed that Paul must have been drinking. "What's the matter?" she asked. "It doesn't seem as if you had a very good time."

"Oh, it's not that," Paul mumbled. "It's just that, when I see all those happy couples, I wonder if I'll ever be like them. I mean, I honestly wonder if I'll ever get married."

"Oh, I'm sure you will," Robert assured him. "Just give it time, that's all."

Give it time, Paul said to himself. How much time? How much time did Paul really have left? He said nothing because he did not want to upset his father. Louise broke Paul's train of thought by bringing up a subject that concerned her even more.

"Paul, you must have had a lot to drink at that wedding," she said, observing her son's tipsy condition.

"Yes, I did. That's what weddings are for, aren't they?"

"I think you'd better lay off the medication tonight son. You know, it's not a good idea to mix pills with alcohol."

"If you say so." Paul did not seem particularly worried.

He sat back in his chair and tilted his head to one side as if he were about to fall asleep. Louise instinctively got up and poured him some coffee from a porcelain pot that was on the table where they were sitting. She set the cup in front of her son.

"Drink some of this, Paul," she suggested. "It'll help perk you up."

Only a few days after Anna had sent it, Paul received her letter. He lay in his bed, holding her handwritten note in his hand. It was a warm, sunny day. Even so, Paul was shut up in his room with the door closed and the curtains pulled. His bedroom was so dark that he lit a lamp over his bed so he could read the letter. Paul preferred obscurity rather than clarity, these days. He no longer wanted to see or hear anything from the outside world. Instead, he desired only to remain in his room.

Paul read the letter twice and then thought about it. Poor kid, he remarked. She's been screwed royally—again! Paul was able to relate Anna's situation to his own, which was, in fact, his sister's intention. The more Paul thought about it, though, the angrier he became. He was angry at many people. He was angry with those students for doing what they did to Anna. He was angry at Anna for letting them get away with it. He was angry at his former colleagues for doing what they did to him. But most of all, Paul was angry with himself. He was angry about letting himself become what he had become.

Ever since that episode at National Exchange, Inc., not to mention the time he had forced himself to take a job he really did not want, Paul felt humiliated and ashamed. Paul's personality was becoming more erratic than ever. Some days, Paul appeared to be kind and docile; on others, he would become frightfully mean and aggressive. It was difficult to pinpoint exactly why this was happening, but apparently it had something to do with the fact that Paul was internalizing all the anger he felt for himself and for others.

Not only was there a problem with his severe mood changes, there were also recent signs that Paul was beginning to hallucinate. He was beginning to create incredible fantasies in his mind about things he really believed that he could do.

The day before he went back to North Carolina, he conjured up another of his impossible dreams. Paul was sitting with his father in the living room, watching television, when he brought up the subject. "You know, Dad," he mentioned. "I think I'm going to be president of the United States one of these days."

"Oh, yeah?" Robert laughed, assuming that Paul was kidding.

"Only I think I'm going to have to change my name," he continued, "because you know that Daleddo is too Italian. Maybe I'll change it to Mom's maiden name."

"Come on, Paul," Robert said with a smirk. "You've got to be putting me on."

Paul's expression changed from casual to severe. "What do you mean by 'Oh, come on?' I'm serious," he insisted. "I'm going to do it. You'll see. The next election, I'm going to run for the presidency, and I'm going to win."

Robert was getting a little worried. "Paul, please tell me you're pulling my leg."

"No, I'm not." Paul was getting more and more defensive, more and more uptight. "I'm not kidding you. I'm not!" "What's the idea of you laughing in my face like that?"

Paul got up from the sofa and approached his father, sitting in a chair on the opposite side of the room. Paul glared down at his father, and Robert stared up at him, cringing in fear. He finally realized that, not only was his son deadly serious, but he was also incredibly hostile toward Robert for not believing him.

"You didn't answer my question, Dad. What's the idea of you laughing in my face like that?" Paul repeated. "I told you that I'm going to be president of the United States, and I mean it. I do mean what I'm saying."

Robert was too afraid to get up from his chair, and too afraid to answer. So he just sat there looking up at Paul with an expression of terror on his face.

"You don't believe me, do you?" Paul continued. "You don't believe that I'm going to be president." Then he took his father by the collar, pulled him up to his feet, and held his fist up to Robert's face. "You're never going to laugh at me like that again."

When he saw that his son was about to strike him, Robert snapped out of his state of inaction and reacted defensively. With one hand, he took hold of Paul's wrist, and with the other, he pushed him away. "Stop, Paul!" he shouted. "You're crazy."

"I'm crazy?" Paul laughed. "I'll teach you to tell me I'm crazy." He took hold of his father by the neck and shook him violently. "I'm not crazy," he shouted. "I tell you I'm not!"

The struggle continued, with Robert trying to free himself from Paul's stranglehold. Suddenly, the door leading to the garage opened. There in the doorway stood Louise, holding two grocery bags in her arms. When she saw what was going on between her husband and son, she set them on a table and hurried over to where they were both fighting.

"Paul, stop!" she shrieked. "Get hold of yourself."

When she saw that Paul was not listening, Louise took her son by the shoulders and pushed him away from his father. Paul stumbled backward, barely avoiding a fall. But once he caught his breath again, he stood straight, staring sheepishly at both of his parents.

"Paul, what's going on with you?" Louise yelled. "Have you lost your mind? What were you doing to your father?"

Paul's harsh expression melted to calmness and sedation. "I-I don't know," he said meekly, shaking his head. "I honestly don't know."

Robert, still shaken by what had happened, looked his son in the eyes. "Have you calmed down, Paul?" he asked him.

"Yes."

Paul was so ashamed and embarrassed by his actions that he could not even look at his parents. Without saying another word, he walked out of the room.

This incident left both of his parents extremely worried about Paul's condition. Not only were they distressed about their son's welfare, they were equally as concerned about their own safety and that of other people around Paul. They realized that if these fits of violence continued, Paul would most surely be a dangerous person to anybody who happened to be near him. So Robert and Louise felt that they had to do something to protect other people, to protect themselves, and—for that matter—to protect their son. What they needed to do, they hadn't a clue.

It happened that the next day, Robert and Louise were talking about this very subject when Paul entered the house.

They were in the kitchen talking over a cup of coffee when he came in the back way. Though Paul came into the house through the family room door, he could hear everything going on in the kitchen.

"Louise," Robert began. "I don't know what we should do about Paul."

"Neither do I," Louise agreed. "I don't know if it's safe to leave him on his own anymore."

"Do you think that we'll have to have him committed again?"

"I hope not. I would never want him to go through that another time."

"But what can we do to keep an eye on him? I certainly wouldn't want anybody to be subjected to his violent behavior. They might call the police on him some day."

"Do you think something like that would happen?"

"You never know. He might get arrested one of these days."

"I don't want to think about it anymore," Louis blurted. "it's a question of what we're going to do in order to keep that from happening."

"There's only one thing I can think to do," Robert said. "We need to contact Dr. Stanton and tell him Paul's condition. I'm sure he'll have an answer."

When he heard this, Paul shuddered. They're going to call Dr. Stanton about me? he thought. If they do that, it won't be long before I end up back in the hospital. Paul was sure of it. He had to react to this decision, and he had to do it fast.

Instead of waiting around for it to happen, he quickly decided to pack his bags and go back to North Carolina. Perhaps that way his parents would understand that telling on him to Stanton would only drive him away.

Paul didn't waste any time. He went to his room, got his suitcase from under his bed, and packed as many clothes into it as he possibly could. Then he went over to his desk and opened the top drawer. He took out all the cash he had in the drawer and put it in his pocket. After he pulled his jacket out of the closet, he picked up his suitcase and slipped out of the house through the back door, got into his car and drove away.

Back in his house in Greensboro, Paul had to face the reality that leaving his parents' house in a state of panic had done him absolutely no good. In fact, he felt worse than ever. Paul knew he was running away from the inevitable. Leaving for Greensboro was not going to keep his parents from doing what they were going to do. His parents might be so concerned that they would call his psychiatrist about him immediately.

Paul felt trapped. He was too scared to make a phone call and too nervous to wait for somebody to call him. Soon enough, though, Paul would find that this problem would resolve itself.

The next day, when Paul was alone in the house, the phone rang. Somehow, Paul knew who it was and why they were calling. "Hello?" he said nervously.

"Hello, Paul? This is Mom."

Paul remained silent for a moment, but then responded. "Hi, Mom," he said softly. "What's up?"

"I think that question should be directed to you," she said. "We've been looking all over for you. We called all of your friends. When we found that you weren't with any of them, we figured you must have gone back to North Carolina. What made you run off like that without telling us?"

"You know what made me do it, Mom," he said. "I didn't like knowing what you wanted to do to me. That's what made me do it."

"Paul, I don't know what you're talking about."

"Don't say that, Mom. You know what you were going to do to me. I overheard you talking about me to Dad right before I left the house. You were going to report me to Dr. Stanton and have him put me back into the hospital."

"Paul," she said. "It wasn't that at all. What we were going to do was tell Dr. Stanton what kind of progress you were making, that's all."

"What kind of progress I was making!" Paul echoed. "You know that's not true. It was just the opposite. You were going to tell Stanton what kind of progress I wasn't making."

"Paul, I'm sorry. All we wanted to do was help you and ourselves. We didn't know that you would get so upset about it."

"What did you expect?" Paul retorted. "Of course, I would get upset about it."

"OK, Paul, We won't say anything to Stanton about you. But are you sure you'll be all right down there?"

"Quite sure," Paul told her. "Aunt Addie knows I'm here, and she said that it was all right."

Now Louise was concerned about Addie's safety as well as everybody else's. "Paul," she said. "Could you do one thing for me?"

"Sure," he consented. "What's that?"

"If you are going to stay down there for any length of time, do keep in touch," she begged him. "Don't let too much time go by without calling us and letting us know how you're doing."

"I'll keep in touch," Paul assured her. "After all, who knows how long I'm going to be down here anyway?"

Louise took that comment to mean that Paul would soon be back in Baltimore. Little did she know that there was a much deeper meaning underlying that statement than she understood right then. Louise decided to end the conversation.

"Take care, Paul," she told him. "I hope I'll be hearing from you soon."

"I'm sure you will be," he promised. "Goodbye, Mom."

Chapter 12

Now that Paul was in North Carolina, he was on his own. In a way, he felt it was good not to be supported by his parents. Nevertheless, he was alone, and this was never a pleasant experience for him. Paul's first order of business was to try to get out and meet people. This was even more important to him than trying to find another job, even though he was running out of money.

The first habit Paul picked up in North Carolina was strolling around the city during the day with not much purpose or foresight of what to expect.

One afternoon when Paul was on his usual stroll, he ran into an interesting display. It was a brightly colored sign in the shape of an arrow with the words, "The Flock Together" painted on it. When Paul looked a little more closely at it, he saw that the arrow pointed to some concrete steps that led down to what was apparently the basement of some building.

Paul went down the steps and arrived at a screen door. When he opened it and reached for the knob of the main door, he noticed that the door was unlocked. So he opened it and went inside.

The place had a "coffee house" type of atmosphere. Some brightly colored "psychedelic" posters hung on the wall, and most of the furniture seemed old and rundown. The place was dimly lit, almost as if somebody were trying to hide something. Most of the clientele looked to be in their late teens or early twenties, with a "punky" appearance. Their hair was long and unkempt, their clothes loud and flashy, and many of them were wearing tattoos. This did not make Paul feel at all ill at ease. He actually felt quite intrigued by these new surroundings.

Not many people were there that day, so Paul wasted no time in finding a table and sitting down. Before long, a young looking girl wearing a flamboyant poncho came up to his table.

"Hi," she greeted him. "How are you doing today?"

"Fine, I guess," he replied. "How are you?"

"Oh, I'm fine," she said. "What can I get you?"

Paul shrugged. "I think I'll have a beer."

"Oh, we don't serve alcohol, here."

"Well, I guess I'll have a cup of coffee then."

"We don't serve coffee, either. As a matter of fact, we don't have anything with caffeine in it. How about a nice, hot barley drink?"

Paul didn't know what that was, but if he couldn't have a beer or a cup of coffee, he had to have something. "OK," he said. "That sounds fine."

In a few moments, the girl returned with a drink that looked to Paul like coffee, but he knew it wasn't. When he took a sip, he found that it didn't taste like much of anything at all. At first, Paul had suspected it, but now he knew that this was a strange place.

"Why on earth don't you sell anything with alcohol or even caffeine in it?" he inquired.

With neither encouragement or invitation, the girl abruptly sat down at the table across from Paul. It was a cinch for Paul to figure that this girl was a little on the bizarre side. He would soon find out that this was an understatement. When Paul looked at her more closely, he realized that she was more than just bizarre. Her shoulder-length blonde hair was frizzy and disheveled. Her skin was extremely pale, she had dark circles around her eyes, and her pupils were so dilated that the color around them could hardly be seen.

"You know," she began as she leaned toward him. "I'm glad you brought that up. We're not here just to please the customers, and we're not even here to make money. We're here to help people."

"Help people," Paul repeated. "Help people with what?"

"We're here to help people find salvation." Her tone seemed intense and serious.

"Salvation? What do you mean by that?"

"Well, we want people to be saved."

"Saved?" Paul asked. "Saved from what?"

"Oh, you must know the answer to that." She shook her head. "Saved from all the ruin and corruption of the world. If you join our fellowship here, I'm sure you will understand where I'm coming from."

Paul laughed to himself. Is this lady for real? he wondered. She was so out in left field that it wasn't even funny. "Look," he told her. "I'm sure that your intentions are good, but I don't think I'm interested in joining any kind of fellowship at this time."

The girl looked at Paul solemnly. "Tell you what," she said. "Feel free to come here any time. On Thursday nights we have live entertainment starting at 8 p.m., and there's no cover charge. I'd be delighted to see you come."

Again, Paul could hardly hide a slight smile. "Thank you," he replied. "But like I said, I'm not in the market for any kind of soul searching or redemption at this particular time."

"Just keep in mind what I said," she said. "The door is open any time. I have the feeling that I'm going to be seeing you again."

Paul didn't respond. Instead, he reached into his back pocket for his wallet. "So how much do I owe you for the coffee? I-I mean, the barley drink?" he stuttered.

"Oh, don't worry about that," the girl said as she smiled. "Like I told you, we're not after anybody's money. We just want to help people."

"Thanks," Paul said. "Maybe next time, the drink will be on me." Then they both got up.

"Don't forget about the Thursday nights here in case you change you mind. They're really a bash."

"OK," Paul agreed. "Thank you again." Paul walked out, convinced he would never return.

But less than a week later, Thursday evening rolled around. Even though Paul had vowed he would never go back to that place, he figured that he had little to lose by checking out the night life there. After all, he did not have a damn thing else to do. So by about 8:30 that night, he left the house to go back to "The Flock Together."

Paul found the place again, strictly by memory. He remembered the area of town it was in, the brightly colored sign in the shape of an arrow, and the concrete steps which led to the basement. Only this time, even before he went in, Paul could hear a loud ruckus coming from the inside.

When he entered the building, he saw that there were at least twice as many people as before. The stage at the front of the room, which had been unoccupied the last time Paul was there, contained a band of four musicians who were playing and singing. Their instruments seemed almost primitive, and their appearance was even more unorthodox. They were all dressed in what looked to Paul like plain white sheets, which were wrapped around their waists and draped over their shoulders. Two of them were shaven completely bald. The sound they were making from their musical instruments was harsh and unsynchronized, to say the least, and their singing was virtually incomprehensible.

Paul knew he should not have come there that night, and when he saw what was going on, he was about to turn and leave without a moment to lose. But as he was headed for the door, who should come up to him but his friend in the poncho.

"Hi, there!" she said excitedly.

Oh, brother, Paul thought. Now he knew he couldn't leave. He was trapped. "Hi, yourself," he said.

"Why don't you have a seat somewhere? I'll go get you something to drink. How about a pomegranate soda?"

Oh, God, Paul shrugged. What is that going to taste like? But at this point he didn't really care. He just wanted to get out of there as soon as possible. "All right," he consented. "That sounds fine."

So the girl left, presumably to get Paul's drink. She had returned so quickly the last time that Paul figured she wouldn't keep him waiting tonight. What he had in the back of his mind was to spend a little time with the girl as he had before and then leave.

At least fifteen minutes passed. Paul finally looked at his watch. What was taking her so long? he wondered. He realized that tonight it was a little busier than the last time he'd been here, but he hadn't even seen the girl waiting on anybody else. As a matter of fact, he hadn't seen her at all since she left his table. About a half hour had passed when Paul decided to leave, drink or no drink. He was about to get up from the table when the girl returned empty-handed.

"Well, don't you have my drink?" Paul asked, looking up at her. Instead of responding, the girl stared at him with an extremely glassy-eyed look. After a few seconds of silence, Paul repeated himself. "Am I going to get a drink, or not?"

It was evident that something was wrong with the girl. "I-I'm sorry." she stuttered. "What did you say?"

Paul was not about to ask the question a third time. Noticing the girl's disoriented condition, he could not help but be concerned. "Are you all right?"

The girl said nothing. Then her head began rocking from side to side. It looked as if she was losing her balance. She grabbed the chair across from Paul and stumbled into it, almost falling to the floor. Her movements were so abrupt that it scared Paul, and he flinched. Then the girl dropped her head and arms on the table.

Paul could not believe what he was witnessing. What was even stranger was that nobody in the place seemed to be paying much attention to what was happening to the girl. Now he knew for sure that he should have never gone back there. Without any further hesitation, Paul got up from the table, hurried over to the main exit and left, vowing never, ever, ever to return.

Paul had already been in North Carolina for several weeks. Once he became bored by loitering around, he made up his mind that he had to go out and get a job. This time, he wasn't at all picky. It was simply a question of keeping busy and making some money at the same time. Paul was trying one last time to build up his life again in North Carolina.

The job Paul had eventually found was with a tobacco company right outside of Greensboro. His job was to cultivate and harvest the tobacco in the fields. Naturally, by comparison to the jobs Paul had had before this one, nothing could have been more degrading to him. Paul was working with what seemed to be the biggest bunch of rednecks and hillbillies he had ever seen in his life. He was poorly paid and was considered strictly a blue collar worker. But since he was running out of money and was unable to find a better job, what else could he do?

By this time it was early May. It was already getting warm in the tobacco fields where Paul was working. His legs were stiff, his arms were sore, and his back ached. He was so exhausted that he felt he had to take a short break to catch his breath. He dropped his shovel on the ground and stretched out. Paul looked up at the sky. His eyes squinted in the sunlight as he cupped his hands over them. Then he looked down again, taking a quick glance at his wristwatch. It was three o'clock. Oh, hell, Paul said to himself. Three more hours in this sweatbox. He felt as if he couldn't go on.

Around six o'clock that evening, an old truck came rattling to where Paul was working. When he heard the noisy horn honk, he threw his shovel on the ground and hurried over to the dirt road where the truck had stopped. He went around to the back of the vehicle and climbed in. Already inside the back of the truck were all the other workmen who had been picked up before him. About half the men were white, and half were black. Almost all of them were clad in blue jeans, plain T-shirts, and heavy work boots. Most of them also had a dirty, uncombed, and untidy appearance.

When Paul joined them in the back of the vehicle, they were all silent. Obviously, they too were tired—almost too tired to speak. As soon as Paul got in and settled, the truck pulled out from the side of the dirt road and drove away.

After about a twenty-minute ride in the truck, they finally arrived at the main building, where the driver pulled into the lot and parked. Here, all of the workmen got out to find their own way home. Paul went directly to the public parking lot, got into his car, and drove away.

One of Paul's many bad habits was driving too fast. He would speed down secondary roads as if they were highways, apparently not caring whether he had an accident or not. Paul had been stopped twice by the police and had been given three points on his license for speeding and reckless driving. This did not seem to deter him from doing what he wanted to do. He kept on zooming down the road, almost as if he wanted to kill himself or somebody else. Today was no exception.

As always, Paul thought that this time he would be able to get away with his reckless behavior and that tomorrow he would slow down and take it easy. Unfortunately, he was wrong. Paul had almost reached the street leading to his house, when he heard a siren coming from a vehicle following close behind him. When he looked in his rear view mirror, he saw that it was a police car with its lights flashing. Oh, no, Paul thought. Not again.

Paul reluctantly pulled his car to the side of the road, while the police car parked directly behind it. When the policeman got out of his car and approached him, Paul noticed that this was the same man who had stopped him the last time. Oh, no, he thought again. Now he was in double trouble.

"Can I see your driver's license, please?" asked the young officer.

Paul hesitantly pulled out his wallet, opened it, and took out his license. He handed it over to the policeman. After he had studied the license carefully, the officer looked back up at Paul. "Didn't I catch you speeding once before in the area?" he asked.

"Yes, you did," Paul confessed.

"As a matter of fact, I think you've already had about three points added to your license for speeding."

"That is right," Paul again admitted.

The cop looked at Paul once more and let out a heavy sigh. "This time I'm going to hold on to your license for a while," he said. "I'm afraid you won't get it back until you've attended a few sessions of Drivers' Rehabilitation."

Paul shrugged. Now what would he do? How would he get to work without being able to drive? His Aunt Addie didn't drive, and the bus lines outside of Greensboro were extremely inefficient. Oh, well. He would just have to call on his Uncle Bobby for some cab service for the time being.

Seeing that Paul looked a little disheartened, the policeman softened his tone. "Come with me, son," he said. "I'll take you down to the station. We can come back and pick up your car later."

This incident with the police and his recent speeding tickets gave Paul an outlook that seemed all the more bleak. Paul's license was revoked, and he was ordered to take eight weeks of Drivers' Rehabilitation if he wanted to get it back.

A few days later Paul quit his job with the tobacco company. Though his uncle would have been more than willing to drive him to and from work until he got his license back, Paul said that he didn't want to bother him that much. This was actually just another feeble excuse for Paul, as sooner or later, he would have quit the job anyway. This kind of work was too physically demanding to continue, and the atmosphere not stimulating enough for him. But since this position was already the bottom of the barrel, the question for Paul was, What else could he possibly do? Where could he go from here? The answer to the question was really quite simple: There was nowhere for him to go.

Actually, it was convenient that Paul happened to be back in North Carolina, because it was at this very time that he was supposed to go see his assigned social worker in Greensboro. Ever since he came out of the hospital, Paul was required to visit with a counselor once a month to make sure he was taking his medicine, holding a steady job, and managing his life appropriately.

Paul was not looking forward to this meeting, as he knew that he would have many less-than-positive things to report. In fact, this time around, he was absolutely dreading it. Nonetheless, Paul knew that if he didn't go see the social worker, he would get into more trouble than if he did go to see him and told the truth. So Paul made up his mind that he would go see his counselor, whether he wanted to or not.

That morning Paul went down to the Social Services Administration in Greensboro. He sat in the main office waiting anxiously for the counselor to come out and call his name. Many other people were waiting there with him. Most of them were men who appeared to be in about the same shape as Paul, except that their appearance made it more evident. Almost all of them were extremely sloppy, with clothes that did not fit right, dirty hair, and unshaven faces. Paul was much more presentable, although his expression was as depressed as theirs, and they all acted as withdrawn and dejected as he did. Not one of them picked up a magazine or newspaper the whole time they were sitting there waiting. They just stared at the walls.

Finally, the counselor came into the waiting room and looked straight at Paul. "Mr. Daleddo," he called out. "I'll see you next."

Paul followed the counselor down the hall and into his office.

"How have you been, Paul?" the counselor asked as he smiled from behind his desk.

"OK, I guess."

"Have you been working these days?"

"I had a job, but I quit."

"You quit?" The counselor seemed surprised. "Why did you quit?"

"Because I didn't have transportation to and from work."

"But you told me the last time you were here that you had a car," the counselor recalled.

"I do," Paul said. "But I lost my license."

"You lost your license?" Now he was even more confused. "How did you do that?"

"I lost it for speeding and reckless driving."

Paul did nothing to hide the truth from the social worker, as he figured that he would find it out sooner or later anyway. After a few moments, the counselor opened a yellow folder that evidently pertained to Paul's case, took a pen from his front pocket, and scribbled something on the pad. Then he looked up at Paul again.

"Paul, have you been taking your medicine regularly?"

Paul became a bit fidgity. "Yes," he said. "I've been taking it."

"What kind of medication are you on?"

"Oh, I don't know the name of it," Paul apologized. "It's something like a strong tranquilizer."

This statement was true. Even when Paul was taking his medicine as prescribed, he never kept track of the names and brands when he changed the medications he was supposed to be taking. But now the situation was even worse, as Paul no longer had a set schedule for taking his medication. He just took it whenever he felt like it.

"You do not know the name of the medicine you are taking?"

"No, but I have the pills at home. The name is right there on the bottle."

The social worker sighed. He took another look down at his case folder and then looked up again. "Paul," he said. "Could you come back to my office this afternoon? I need to see you one more time today."

A cold child ran down Paul's spine. This was the first time a social worker had ever asked him to come back during the same day. What was worse, the social worker sounded serious this time. It's bad news, Paul thought. He was sure that he was really going to get it this time. Paul was so scared he did not dare to ask why the social worker wanted to see him again that day. So he simply answered the man's question. "Of course, I can come back this afternoon. At what time would you like to see me?"

"Oh, I'd say around two," said the counselor. "There's no rush. You can come back when you've finished your lunch."

"That sounds fine," Paul said. "I guess I'll be seeing you in a couple of hours." Before the counselor had time to respond, Paul got up from his chair and left the office, closing the door abruptly behind him.

As soon as he was outside, Paul took a quick look at the sky and then down at his watch. Eleven o'clock. Three more hours to live. Now Paul was so nervous that he couldn't think of eating anything. He decided to pass these three miserable hours by walking around on the traffic-heavy streets of Greensboro.

After three lonely hours of pacing the streets and side-walks of the city, two o'clock finally rolled around. By then Paul was so overwrought with all his idle worry that he could barely drag himself back to the building. His heart was pounding as he returned to the main office and sat down in the waiting room. In a way, he wanted this over with—in a way, he didn't. Paul had a strong instinct that when he finished with this second encounter, he would feel much worse than before he went into it.

Soon the counselor stepped into the waiting room again. He said nothing but motioned for Paul to come with him to his office. They walked down the hall and sat down in their respective chairs.

"Paul," the counselor said. "I've discussed your case with the director of this office, and we both feel that you haven't made sufficient progress since you were released from Carolina State Hospital. We think that you may have to go back into the hospital if you don't improve quickly."

Again, Paul felt a cold chill run through his body. "What do you mean by 'improving very quickly?'" he asked.

"What I mean is that you will be put on two weeks' probation. Within that time, you'll be required to find a steady job and get an official report signed by a physician about the medication you are taking. We would also like to see you work on getting your driver's license back. If you are unable to do this within the amount of time stated, you will have to go back into the hospital."

Paul's expression turned to one of unbearable distress, but all he knew to do was to respond to the most current circumstances. "Well," he replied. "I'll do what I can."

Paul didn't have anything more to say to the social worker, so he just got up to leave again. Not knowing what else to do, he shook hands with the counselor, thanked him for seeing him that afternoon, and walked away. As Paul headed for the door, the social worker reminded him one more time of what he had said before.

"Remember, Paul," he called out to him. "You've got two weeks to straighten things out. Good luck to you." Paul nodded his head as he walked out of the office.

Paul thought about this development while he was standing outside waiting for the bus. Two weeks, he repeated. That was not enough time. Paul knew damn well that he would not be able to straighten everything out in two weeks. He decided he would have to make a definitive decision quickly. He needed to do something that would resolve everything, once and for all. Deep inside, Paul knew what that "something" was, though he still could not admit it even to himself. Soon enough, though, Paul would come to grips with the harsh reality of it all. He would realize that suicide was the best solution for him.

Chapter 13

The aspect of life that perturbed Anna most about the whole Arabic mentality was how some of them seemed to cast themselves highly above everyone else. The actual wealth of the entire country appeared to be very poorly distributed. It seemed to Anna as if 10 percent of the population in that country held 90 percent of the wealth. While some citizens lived like princes, most existed like paupers. While some drove fancy French sports cars, most went everywhere by foot. While some lived in mansions, most were obligated to live in huts rather than houses.

As if this were not unjust enough, Anna was unnerved by the way the wealthy people in the country seemed able to pay their way out of anything, even the most serious crimes. They knew the cops, the lawyers, and the judges who could help them weasel out of almost any misdoing.

Even more shocking to Anna was the way these people liked to brag about having access to special privileges. Two particular incidents reinforced this impression on Anna's part. Each was a personal encounter with Tunisians who seemed to be leading an unscrupulous way of life.

One incident happened when a man, probably about thirty years of age, had the gall to try to pick Anna up as she was walking to and from the Institute. It was bad enough that this fellow was married and did not try to hide it, but his demeanor was such that he seemed to have no shame about anything at all. The first few times he approached Anna, she stopped to talk to him for a few moments, and after several persistent invitations, she agreed to have a cup of coffee with him.

As Anna sat in the café and chatted with him, she found that he seemed to have a good job which earned him a fairly good income, but he did not have a car. This surprised her, as she knew that most of the well-to-do people in that country took pride in owning a vehicle, so she asked him why this was so.

The man confessed that he was not comfortable driving because he had hit and killed a pedestrian one time. He readily admitted that the accident was his fault because he had been driving in an inattentive and reckless manner that day, but he seemed to show no remorse as he recounted the story. Then, when Anna him if there were any repercussions for his actions, he said that positively no action was taken against him. The reason for this, he said, was that one of the policeman at the scene of the accident was an uncle and that some of his family members were able to influence the judge who handled that case. After this, Anna decided not to associate with the man any more.

The second time Anna heard an story like this was when she'd been invited to two of her students' home for lunch. Two sisters boasted that their father had a high position in the ministry of foreign affairs. Anna doubted to herself whether that was true. Then both of the young ladies admitted that they were not at their best that day, because it happened that their brother was in jail. They said that the potential charge was "driving while intoxicated" and "involuntary manslaughter."

It seemed that this young man, while driving drunk, had been involved in an accident that had killed somebody. Even though the two girls were not themselves that day, they told Anna that they were confident that their brother would get off, because their father had already made arrangements with court officials to twist the story in the young man's favor. Anna was certain that these "arrangements" had something to do with money or even bribes.

Both of these incidents were still fresh in Anna's mind. In fact, it seemed as if she thought about them day and night. Anna was so preoccupied that one afternoon in her apartment Noureddine felt compelled to ask her what it was.

"Annie," he began. "What's the matter?"

"Oh," Anna sighed. "I was thinking about a couple of things some people told me a while back."

"What kind of things?"

"It's sort of complicated," Anna explained. "But to make a long story short, a couple of guys each killed somebody due either to reckless or drunk driving, and they both got off scot-free because their families knew the right people."

"Did this happen here?"

"Of course," Anna declared. "These people live right here in Tunis." Then she looked at Noureddine with a sober expression. "How could they possibly have gotten away with something like that?"

"Annie," Noureddine laughed. "You have not heard the half of it."

"What do you mean?"

"Just what I said, Annie. The situation is much worse than you could ever have imagined. That's why the attitudes among the common people are as they are."

"How are the attitudes among the common people?" Anna asked.

This made Noureddine laugh. "Don't play dumb with me," he told her. "You remember that mass demonstration last year that I told you about?"

"Yes."

"I saw people die with my own eyes. I saw people slaughtered who wanted only justice and equality for everyone. Is that too much to ask for?"

"Of course not. But the government didn't want that, so they killed the people. Though one of these days, they will pay for the misery they've caused. You'll see."

Anna was getting the impression that there was something Noureddine was not telling her. "How will they pay for what they've caused?" she inquired.

"We have our ways of making them pay," Noureddine said. "We'll get even one of these days."

At this Anna began to feel more and more uneasy. "You sound as if you've got something up your sleeve," she told him. "Would you mind telling me what it is?"

"Annie," Noureddine said hesitantly. "You probably wouldn't want to know what it is that I have up my sleeve. It's something you've probably never encountered before in your life."

Anna shuddered. The more she was with Noureddine, the more she was learning about him. Anna was determined to get to the bottom of this matter once and for all. She realized that if she didn't, she would never know the truth about this person who had become all too important to her.

"What are you trying to tell me?" she asked him, speaking in a soft voice.

"Don't worry about it, Annie," Noureddine said. "Like I said, you probably wouldn't want to know about it anyway."

Anna was becoming more curious by the moment. "Noureddine," she said, "tell me what it is. You know that you can't leave me wondering like this."

"All right," Noureddine said, turning toward her. "If you want to know the truth, I'll tell it to you." Then he turned away again. "You see, a couple of years ago, some of my friends and I got together and formed our own underground political group."

"What kind of political group?" asked Anna.

"A revolutionary group—one that wants political change."

"A revolutionary group?" Anna knew that this could mean different things to different people. "What is that supposed to mean?"

"Just what I said, Annie," Noureddine said. "It's a group that wants political change. It is one that wants equality for everyone."

Anna was beginning to understand. "It is enough," she said, "but how do you expect to obtain this equality?"

"We have our ways," Noureddine informed her. "Now we're waiting for when the time is right."

"When do you think that will be?"

"Soon enough," Noureddine stated. "Now it's only a question of something starting which will allow us to move into the political scene."

The more Anna talked to Noureddine, the more she realized that this was not just a revolutionary group—it was more like an organization of militants or even terrorists. God knows what they would do if they did get into power. And after all this, Noureddine wanted to come to the United States to live? Anna had no idea of what she might be getting herself into.

"Let me ask you one thing, Noureddine. When this opportunity arises, how do you and your group plan to exploit it?"

"In many different ways," Noureddine responded. "We will use it and abuse it, if need be. We will lie and cheat and steal—"

"—And even kill?"

"And even kill."

Anna was almost speechless. Did Noureddine really mean what he was saying, or was he just trying to appear tough and indestructible? When the time came, would he really follow through with the actions he had just been talking about? Even if this were some kind of pretense, it was a cruel and sinister one, not to be taken lightly in any case.

Anna could not imagine what a future with a man like this would be, so she found herself unable to talk about it. Instead, she remained silent, looking as hostile and opposing as she possibly could. Noticing this, Noureddine finally came around and questioned her, not realizing that it would soon start the most serious argument they had ever had.

"Annie," Noureddine said, seeing her look so grim. "What's up?"

Anna did not answer him. Rather than attacking him verbally, she got up and stormed out of the apartment. Slamming the door as she walked out, Anna went out into the hallway and stood there, leaning against the iron railing and staring down at the stairs of the building. Soon afterward, Noureddine followed her out of the apartment and found her standing in the hallway.

"I think you know what's up," Anna said. "I don't like the conversation that we just had."

For the first time since they had started this discussion, Noureddine acted a little ashamed. "Annie," he said softly. "Why don't we go back inside? I don't care to discuss it out here." When Anna nodded her head, they both went back into the apartment.

As soon as they were inside and had sat down, Anna started the debate. "You must understand how I feel about this," she declared. "I don't like it at all."

"I knew you wouldn't," Noureddine agreed. "That's why I didn't want to tell you."

"It gives me the creeps, Noureddine," Anna blurted out. "It gives me the creeps to think that the man I might marry is a revolutionary."

"Marry?" Noureddine raised his eyebrows. "Who said anything about marriage?"

Anna's expression changed from concerned to astonished. "I thought that was what you had in mind," she said. "I thought that was why you wanted to come to the United States."

"That's not necessarily the case," Noureddine said. "What I meant was that I wanted to go there to travel."

"You mean that you only wanted to go there for a visit?" Anna was shocked.

Noureddine didn't know how to answer her. "Not exactly," he said. "I might consider living there someday, but I think that the idea of marriage is yet to be seen."

Needless to say, Anna did not like the direction of this conversation, and she especially didn't care for Noureddine's ambiguity about the matter of their getting married. But she figured that the best idea was to get to the bottom of the issue, once and for all. Anna decided to clarify any question regarding her relationship with Noureddine.

"I think it's time to clear up any misconceptions we have right now, Noureddine," she said. "What exactly do you expect out of this relationship?"

"I don't know," he shrugged. "What do you expect out of it?"

The more Anna talked to Noureddine, the more unnerved she became. She couldn't understand why he was being so vague and uncertain. "I don't know what your intentions were," she told him. "But I assumed since you invited me to visit your family that you were serious about me."

"I am serious about you, but I just don't know about marriage. There's more that concerns me about our relationship right now than there is regarding what's going to happen later on." He hesitated a few seconds as if he were thinking of something quick to say. "For instance," he remarked, "why are you always defying me in front of other people?"

"Defying you?" uttered Anna. "What the hell are you talking about?"

"I'm talking about the other day when you were at my place, and a couple of my friends were there, and you kept calling me a liar."

"A liar?" Anna exclaimed. "When did I call you a liar?"

"You didn't call me a liar as such," Noureddine admitted. "But you kept insisting that what I was saying was not true."

"Oh, yeah," Anna recalled. "What I meant was that you were joking. You know that I would never call you a liar."

"But it's the same thing."

"It's not the same thing." Anna felt exasperated. She realized that they had gotten completely off the subject they had been talking about before, and Anna was sure that Noureddine had done it on purpose. They started out by talking about the crucial subject of crime and politics, then switched to their future plans, and now had transformed their discussion into a trivial argument. How could she have let something like that happen? Anna thought.

"I don't know how we got into this, but I know one thing," she told Noureddine. "I know how I feel about the idea of marriage, but you don't seem to feel the same way. You don't want it at all." Anna burst into tears and began weeping.

When he saw how upset Anna had become, Noureddine almost felt guilty. Almost. "Annie, ANNIE. Don't cry," he begged. "I didn't mean that I did not want to go to the United States. All I meant was that we have certain compatibility problems that need to be ironed out first."

"Compatibility problems or no compatibility problems, it doesn't matter any more," Anna sobbed. "You don't want to marry me, and that's all there is to it."

"Annie," he said half heartedly. "I told you from the start that I wanted to go to the United States, and of course I'm thinking of going there to live someday. But for now, I feel that we have to work things out between the two of us before we could possibly think about marriage."

"What things are we going to have to work out?" Anna asked, her words flavored with the bitter taste of sarcasm.

"You know what I mean," Noureddine insisted. "Certain aspects of our relationship need to be worked out."

"Would you mind explaining that a little further?"

Noureddine felt as if he had been put on the spot. "I hadn't given it much thought," he answered meekly. "But I know that there are things that need to be changed."

This aggravated Anna even more, as she knew that Noureddine was deliberately trying to evade the issue and to make excuses for himself. "I know better than you what changes need to be made," she said sharply. "These are changes that are going to have to be made in you."

"In me," Noureddine echoed. "How do you figure that?"

"I'm beginning to think that you're too much of a militant for me," Anna declared.

Noureddine almost laughed out loud. "A militant?" he mocked. "What's that supposed to mean?"

"It means that you're too politically biased and too dictatorial."

"So do you think that you're so perfect?"

"Of course not," Anna replied. "But at least I'm not a communist."

Noureddine was not expecting such an abrupt remark. Still, he didn't argue. "So what of it?" he said. "Is that the worst thing you can be?"

"No," Anna said. "The worst thing that you can be is a terrorist. I believe in equality for all the world just as much as you do, but I'm not about to lie, cheat, steal—and kill—for it."

For the first time since they had started this conversation, Noureddine felt downright degraded. Even though he knew that she wouldn't approve of his ideas, it had never crossed his mind that she would defy him as she did. Noureddine felt that he had to compromise in some shape, form, or fashion. "How about if we forget the whole thing?" he suggested.

"Forget the whole thing? How do we do that? How do we forget something that concerns our future?"

"I don't mean 'forget' in the true sense of the word," Noureddine explained. "What I mean is to put the idea off for the time being. Otherwise, we'll be so preoccupied with the future that we won't be able to think about what's going on right now."

"You're right," Anna granted. "Maybe it would be better if we forgot about it. I'm sure that these differences of opinion will be resolved sooner or later."

"I'm sure they will be."

For the rest of the day Anna thought about that conversation. Was it worth worrying about? Indeed, it was. If this all-too-close companion of hers really was a communist or terrorist, where did she fit into this arrangement? If it were true, why would she want to marry him at all? The answer was quite simple. Anna loved Noureddine too much not to want to spend the rest of her life with him. Yet after all this, Noureddine had left her with the impression that he didn't want to marry her at all. Anna felt she had been double-crossed by Noureddine, first by who he was, and then by what he had done to her. Still, she couldn't let go of him now. Anna wanted to spend the rest of her life with Noureddine, whether it turned out to be the best thing for her or not.

The next day Anna took a walk up to the Souks to do a little shopping for her apartment after work. On her way back, she passed through an area near the Medina. She was approached by a woman she had seen in the city before. The woman held out her hand and mumbled something in Arabic. She was obviously a beggar, undernourished, dirty, and draped in a huge cloth which Anna was sure was a bed sheet. She was also carrying a very small child in her arms.

Anna was never the kind to patronize solicitors, either in her own country or abroad. She always thought that if a person couldn't support himself, it was his tough luck, so normally she would turn this type of person away. Still, there was something about this woman that touched her today. After a few seconds of contemplation, she reached into her purse and pulled out some change. The woman smiled with gratitude as Anna put it in her hand. Then she continued on her way.

When Anna got to the doorstep of her apartment, she was encountered by another needy creature—a small cat, totally black, and obviously very hungry. Anna had noticed since she had been there that there seemed to be a problem with pet overpopulation, as they seemed to run free and unattended everywhere. Furthermore, none of them appeared very well cared for. Anna tried to get past this poor little menace, but he meowed so much that she could not bring herself to leave him like that. So she reached into a bag with some food that she had bought while shopping at the Souks and pulled out a sandwich. Inside was a piece of chicken that Anna figured she could part with. She lay it down on the step so that the poor beast could feast on it. Then she went inside.

After she got into her apartment, Anna thought about what had just happened. It was not like her to be so generous. What made her change today? Perhaps it was all the injustice she had been witnessing since she had been in this country, or perhaps it was the conversation that had taken place between her and Noureddine the night before.

Whatever the reason, maybe it was causing Anna to change for the better. Maybe she was becoming less self serving and egocentric. That afternoon, Anna thought about it some more. Homeless cats and homeless humans, she thought. In the United States there would be shelters for both.

Chapter 14

The end of the school year at the Institute was approaching, and the students would soon be taking their final exams. Unlike the mid-year English language examinations, however, this would not consist of just a written test. The students would also be taking oral exams in order to evaluate their verbal mastery of the language they had been studying. This meant that the teachers would be busier than ever, because there would be a ratio of one teacher to each student during the evaluation process. Anna was excited about this new duty, as she had never performed a task such as this and concluded that it would be challenging. Also, she felt that it was her last chance to prove that she had any worth there at the establishment.

Soon it would be time for the schedule for the oral exams to be posted in the teachers' room. The names of the teachers in the English department and all the days and times they worked would be listed.

Anna returned to the teachers' room before leaving the Institute that afternoon to see if it had been completed. Indeed it had. There it was on the wall.

Anna went up to what looked like a chart, with many names filling different time slots for the different days of the week. She looked at the schedule closely. Much to her surprise, she could not find her name on it anywhere. She looked again to make sure she wasn't mistaken, but the result was the same. Her name was nowhere to be found.

Soon after, a colleague of hers came in. This English gentleman went up to where Anna was standing to take a look at the schedule. He found his name on it immediately. Then he turned to Anna. "When is your turn to do this?" he inquired in a nonchalant manner.

"I don't seem to be up there," Anna responded.

Then the man looked up at the schedule again, this time more thoroughly. "You're not," he said, sounding just as surprised Anna was.

Not only was it shocking to Anna that she was excluded from the entire project, but what was even more disparaging was that she seemed to be the only one who had not been asked to participate. It appeared to Anna that the name of every teacher in the English department was on that schedule but hers. Anna was sure that this was being done on purpose. Once again, the administration must have decided that Anna probably was unable to handle such a responsibility. In a way, Anna could not blame them. With her track record at the job, wouldn't anybody have come to that conclusion?

Anna gathered her things and walked out of the teachers' room. She went downstairs and proceeded to leave the Institute. As she was doing so, she thought about it. How long would she last? she questioned. How long could her mind and soul endure such insult and degradation? The answer would come to her sooner than she thought.

Since it was almost the end of the year, and since Anna seemed to be of so little use to anybody there, she thought that she might get a break. She thought that everybody at the Institute might stop leaning on her, but this was not the case. They were not going to give an inch—not even now. But the problem was that Anna did not become completely aware of this until she was approached by the same female coordinator who had given her so much trouble at the beginning of the year.

"Miss Daleddo," the woman said in her normal overbearing voice. "Could you please make a copy of your schedule, marking down what classes you have and where they are, and would you mind turning it into Mr. Ben Hassen as soon as possible?"

"Of course, I wouldn't mind," Anna replied, having no idea why the coordinator was asking for this.

Anna assumed that this was a general procedure for all the teachers, but that was only a guess. So that afternoon she made a neat little chart with all her classes, showing exactly when and where they were. Then she took her schedule and went up to Ben Hasten's office to give it to him.

"Hello," she said as she entered his office. "I understand that you wanted to see a copy of my schedule."

Ben Hassen sat up straight at his desk when he saw Anna come in. "Yes, I did."

"Here it is." Anna walked up to Ben Hassen's desk and presented him with the schedule.

Ben Hassen looked it over carefully. "There," he pointed. "That's the class I'm looking for. I went down there the other day and saw a lot of dirt and litter in the classroom."

It was true. That group was probably the worst-behaved of all of Anna's classes. It was getting to the point where they would bring in peanuts and sunflower seeds, and sometimes they would even carry soft drinks into class with them. Then they would leave the bottles on their desks and drop the shells all over the floor. Now that the administration was beginning to take notice of this, they were tracing it back to Anna as her own responsibility. How terribly embarrassing, she thought. At this point, she didn't care.

"Mr. Ben Hassen," Anna addressed him. "You know that they're my worst group. Now you know when and where their class is. So all you have to do is go down there when they're carrying on like that and tell them to stop."

Anna meant every word. She'd figured that if Ben Hassen wanted a complete schedule of Anna's classes, it meant that he wanted to go there and check things out for himself. If he didn't take care of the problem, then it would have to stay the way it was. Anna was not intimidated by what Ben Hassen was saying to her. She knew that it was almost the end of the year and that whatever was going to happen would happen—and that was the extent of it.

Ben Hassen thanked her for the schedule, and Anna left the office.

It took only a few days for Anna to get some feedback from the information she had earlier provided for Ben Hassen. Later on that week, she went back to his office and was greeted right away with a reprimand. He told her that he had gotten another complaint about the mess the class had left in the room that morning. When he saw her the next day, it was even worse. Ben Hassen told her that one of the chairs in the back of the room was found broken. He also threw in that this was first time in the history of the Institute that something like this had happened. So what? Anna thought. There's got to be a first time for everything.

It was unlike Anna not even to try to rectify a situation. Once she had reacted to their misbehavior by going over to one of the students, taking all the peanuts off of his desk, and throwing them across the room. Although it stunned the class for a few seconds, it did not stop any of them from continuing to munch and drink away. Another time, when she saw one of the girls sipping a soda during class, Anna kindly asked her to refrain from doing so. When the student refused, she stopped the class and charged right up to the administrative office. Anna found one of the technicians there and asked him to come down with her to help straighten out the predicament. In a few moments after he went down with her, the class settled down, and the girl stopped her antics, but again, it lasted only a few moments. As soon as the technician left, they were back to their old tricks.

Anna was trapped. She knew that it was far too late to change the patterns she had established earlier that year. At the same time, she was expected to make every effort to discipline the students as she was supposed to have been doing all along. As far as Anna was concerned, the only thing she could hope for was to survive the school year with her job and sanity intact. An easy feat, one would think. Little did Anna know, however, that the events taking place right now were leading to quite a different outcome.

By now, Anna had caught on that the whole idea of having her make a schedule of all her classes was to try to sabotage her. They were trying to prove that it was her fault that certain classrooms were left looking like pigpens. Yet despite the fact that they had their reasons for doing what they did, Anna considered it to be nothing more than a despicable trick. She knew all along that they must have suspected that it was her classes that were littering up the rooms, so why didn't they just ask her about it? As always, Anna felt resentful toward the administration for doing this, but what could she do? Again, she knew that it was entirely too late to correct the mistakes she had made at the beginning of the year. Now she could only wait for the end to come, and before she knew it, it would.

Ben Hassen considered himself too busy a man to trouble himself with any problems that Anna was supposed to take care of herself. But while Anna had to answer to Ben Hassen, he in turn had to answer to the director, who always seemed to leave his second-in-command with the dirty work. Ben Hassen felt that he had to tell the director about what was going on with Anna's classes, or he would be held responsible for it. Being on the insecure side, Ben Hassen left any important decisions to his superior. So any time there was a problem, he would always run to the director to find out what to do. This was exactly what he was planning to do about Anna. He was going to deal with her in the same way he would deal with any problem of this kind. He would take it straight to the director.

The next day Ben Hassen made a phone call to the director. The director, sitting at his desk at the time, picked up the phone. "Hello?" he responded.

"Hello. It's Ben Hassen. I need to talk to you about something urgent," he said.

"If it's urgent, come to my office right away," the director replied.

"OK."

In an instant Ben Hassen was in the director's office. He sat in one of the low-seated chairs in front of the director's desk. These chairs conveniently made the director look bigger and taller than anybody else sitting in his office.

"What seems to be the problem, Ben Hassen?" he said as he sat back in his high-seated, swivel chair.

"It's that Miss Daleddo again. You knew that she's been having trouble all along, don't you?"

"Yes, I knew," the director said in a half-disgusted tone of voice.

"Now she's letting her students destroy this building," Ben Hassen said. "Yesterday a chair was found broken, and before that, bottles and nutshells were found all over the floor in her classroom."

The director became so angry he was speechless. This was certainly not the first time he had gotten a complaint about Anna. This was positively the last straw.

"What's more, she doesn't seem terribly concerned about what her students are doing," Ben Hassen added. "When I tell her these things, she just shrugs her shoulders and walks away."

The director went from angry to furious. Who does this lady think she is? he thought. Are we paying her for nothing? But he still did not verbally react to what he had been told.

When Ben Hassen saw the director's stern expression, it almost made him scared. "So what do we do?" he asked, trying to break up this aura of rigidity.

"I think you know what we must do," the director said coldly. "That girl has got to go. That is all there is to it."

"Do you mean that we must fire her?" Ben Hassen said, sounding a bit shocked.

"That is exactly what I mean," the director announced. "I've given the girl several warnings concerning her incompetence. Now we are perfectly within our rights to do what we must do."

"I suppose you're right," Ben Hassen granted. "But are you positive you should take such drastic measures?"

"Now is as good a time as any," the director presumed. "If she hasn't made any progress this year, she surely isn't going to make any progress next year. In that case, I don't want her coming back after summer vacation."

Ben Hassen sighed. "It's up to you, but how do we go about doing it?"

"There's no problem," the director confirmed. "All I have to do is call the superintendent and recommend that Miss Daleddo be terminated. Once the decision has been made, he will then write her a letter telling her this, and you can give it to her."

Ben Hassen couldn't believe his ears. "I'm going to give her the letter?" he gasped.

"Yes, you will do it," the director nodded. "You know, you're always the one who handles public relations."

Public relations? Ben Hassen repeated to himself. He considers this a matter of public relations? Ben Hassen considered it more of a cut-throat action. That girl was going to get the axe, and he was the one who was going to have to carry the axe to her. Oh, God, Ben Hassen thought. Why did the director always stick him with these jobs?

"I-I wasn't expecting to have to do that," he stuttered. "After all, it's your decision to fire her."

"But you're the one who brought it up in the first place," the director said. "Can't you follow through with what you just said?"

Ben Hassen felt a little embarrassed by his obvious lack of courage. "I guess so," he said. "I will do it."

"Very good," the director said. "As soon as I get the letter from the superintendent, you can give it to Miss Daleddo."

"All right."

After Ben Hassen had thanked the director for seeing him that day and vice versa, they shook hands and bade each other good day. Then Ben Hassen left his office.

Walking back to his own office, Ben Hassen almost felt guilty. Almost. Poor kid, he thought. She was going to get the axe, and it would be partially his fault. But what else could he have done? Ben Hassen had to tell the director, otherwise he would have been held accountable for everything Anna was doing. So now he was free from all blame. After all, it was the decision of the director to fire Anna, so that was entirely his responsibility. But the problem was that Ben Hassen was left with the job of telling her this. Oh, God, he thought. How did he ever let himself get into such a mess? For the rest of the day, Ben Hassen sat alone in his office, feeling like an ogre and a do-gooder at the same time.

At the time of the final exams, Anna would at last meet her fate. This was a particularly tedious job for her, because she was scheduled to work only as a substitute. This meant she would only proctor an exam if the regularly scheduled teacher did not show up. Again, Anna considered this to be a personal insult, as it meant to her that they did not need her at all. But she had not yet seen the half of it.

Anna was sitting alone in the teachers' room, waiting impatiently for somebody not to show up, when Ben Hassen approached her. "Are you supposed to be substituting today?" he asked in a subdued voice.

"Yes, I am," she answered.

"Come with me," he told her. "I have a class taking a test where there's no teacher."

Oh, wow, Anna said to herself. This was her big chance. She was finally being asked to do something, now that it was almost the end of the school year. After Ben Hassen had picked up the stack of exams on the table, Anna followed him up to the classroom where the test was being given.

Ben Hassen set all of the tests on the front desk and politely pulled the chair out for Anna to sit down. "I'll pass out the exams myself," he said. "All you have to do is stay with the students until the exam is over."

Anna looked up at Ben Hassen as she sat down at her desk. "What time is this test over?" she asked him.

"At noon," he answered.

At noon, she repeated to herself. It was nine o'clock in the morning. Oh, brother, she thought. She had three hours in that classroom with nothing to do except babysit a bunch of brain-racked students. Oh, well, she thought. At least she was being asked to do something.

Finally, noon rolled around, and Ben Hassen came back to the room to collect all the exams. Once he had the tests together, Anna thought for sure that he would dismiss her right away. However, he didn't. Instead, he hit her with a most unexpected question.

"Could you stop by my office before you leave today?" he requested.

"Of course," Anna responded. She didn't dare ask him the reason for this. As soon as she nodded, Ben Hassen walked out of the classroom.

Oh, no, Anna thought. Today was the day. Anna was sure that on this day something extremely significant was going to happen. And she could tell by Ben Hassen's subdued and preoccupied demeanor that when she went to see him, it was going to be very bad news. So Anna elected to get herself into Ben Hassen's office as soon as she could, before she lost her nerve.

Anna left the classroom and went down to Ben Hassen's office. She opened the door and walked in. "Yes?" she greeted him. "What did you want to see me about?"

"It's about this," Ben Hassen replied.

When Anna approached his desk, Ben Hassen handed her a typewritten letter which read as follows:

I regret to inform you that it has been decided to put an end to your services starting from the commencement of the next scholastic year.

As a consequence of this decision, your contract of recruitment no. 67 will cease to have effect beginning from the time mentioned in the above paragraph of this letter.

Sincerely,
Salem Zemiri
Superintendent of the Universities of Tunis

Anna stood there, not knowing what to say or do. She understood exactly what the superintendent was telling her in this letter, but she still did not know how to react. Anna felt she had no choice but to be certain of the meaning of the letter with Ben Hassen.

"This means that I will not be working here next year," she said, not as a question, but as a statement.

"No, you will not be working here," Ben Hassen said, looking straight ahead and not at Anna.

Anna felt nothing but shock. In spite of the fact that in a way she had anticipated this all along, she felt so stunned she could hardly speak. Anna demanded no explanation and offered no argument with her supervisor. She just left. She stormed out of Ben Hassen's office, leaving the door flying open behind her.

Chapter 15

Darlene sat alone in her home in New York City peacefully reading the newspaper when the phone rang. She tossed the paper onto a nearby table, got up from the sofa, and went to the kitchen to answer it. The phone rang several times before she picked it up.

"Hello?"

"Hello. Who is this?"

"It's Darlene. Who is this?"

"It's Paul."

"Oh, hi, Paul. Where are you?"

"I'm living down in North Carolina."

"Oh, yeah. Your parents—"

"Hey, listen, Darlene. You've got to help me. It's really important."

"What's important?"

"I've got to talk to Steve (Darlene's husband). He's got to help me get into med school next year."

"Med school? Since when?"

"Or maybe I can get in touch with Andy. Maybe he can help me apply to Harvard Law School this coming fall."

"Harvard Law School?"

"Hey, Darlene. What about your father? Is he still working with computers? Maybe the two of us can start a business together."

"But I thought—"

"Listen, Darlene. You've got to help me. Because soon it'll be too late."

"Too late? But Paul, I don't understand."

"Darlene—Darlene!"

She heard a sigh and a moan, and then a click from the telephone. They were soon cut off. Darlene stared at the telephone for a few seconds. Then she slowly reached up to the wall and hung it up. What was this all about? she wondered. Could it have been some sort of joke? It crossed Darlene's mind that Paul and some of the other cousins might have decided to get together and play a gag on her. But no, she told herself. They wouldn't do something like that. But what was with Paul to ramble on like that? Could he have been on something? Probably not, she concluded. Paul had been fine the last time she saw him. But really—what was the problem with him? And what was all this about being "too late"?

Only Paul would have the answers to these questions. Darlene was one of his many paternal cousins. She was also one of those competitive relatives with whom he dared not try to be a rival. Yet she was not the only one. Andy was another cousin Paul cared not to contend with. These peers of his offered him nothing but feelings of inadequacy. But the ironic thing about it was that now, he was trying desperately to reach out to them. He had already made other phone calls to his different relatives in New York, and they were all basically of the same nature as this one. So Paul had the desire to communicate with all of his paternal cousins again. Yet all along, Paul was right. It really was too late.

For the past several years, Paul had avoided that side of the family, because he did not like the competition and jealousy (including his own) that he saw among them. He only visited them when he had to, on special and infrequent occasions. Now he wanted to get in with them again. But again, all along, Paul was right. It really was too late.

A few days before the episode over the phone with Darlene, Paul had stopped taking his medicine. When he was with his parents, Robert and Louise tried to see that Paul took his medicine when he was supposed to. Since Paul had returned to North Carolina, however, they were not there and could not oversee this responsibility.

Ever since his breakdown, the medication that Paul had been taking regulated his entire body system, calmed his nerves, and kept his mind reasonably clear and coherent. It did all this for Paul, but with almost unbearable side effects. Now Paul wanted to be free from everything. Only he wasn't. Paul was even more imprisoned by his mental disorder than before. So this confirmed even more his decision that suicide was the best solution.

Paul, basically a precise and methodical person, had already thought of various ways of killing himself. An overdose was one possibility, but it was far too dangerous, as it often did the job only halfway. The same was true of carbon monoxide poisoning, or even jumping from tall buildings. So for Paul, there was only one surefire way of doing the away with himself—the good old revolver. It was quick, easy, and safe, when done correctly. Paul was certain this was how he wanted to do it. So now it was merely a question of getting hold of the weapon.

Paul had two weeks. He had only that amount of time to do what he needed to do. After that, it would be too late. So it was of utmost importance to Paul to get his hands on a gun—legally or illegally—in time. Then he remembered the girl he had met in that basement less than a month ago. That young lady struck him as the type who might have access to such weapons. He didn't bother to recall that he had vowed twice never to return to that poor excuse for a hangout. But desperate situations call for drastic measures. Paul decided to go back to that fluky place to try to track down that girl.

This time when Paul went to the city of Greensboro, he drove rather than taking the bus. Paul hadn't gotten his license back, but he figured at this point that it didn't really matter what he did anyway. Once he got to town, Paul immediately found the street where the place was located. When he pulled up and parked beside the building, he once again noticed the brightly colored sign in the shape of an arrow with the words "The Flock Together" written on it. He got out of his car, walked down the concrete steps, and opened the screen door.

When he tried to turn the knob of the main door, he discovered it was locked. As this surprised and confused him, Paul peered through the window to find out what was going on. The place seemed completely deserted. All the tables had been moved into a corner of the room, with the chairs on top of them. It was dark inside except for one light shining down on the stage in the front of the room. Paul could not believe his eyes. Had the place gone out of business? he wondered. Or had it just closed down temporarily for some renovation? Oh, well, Paul thought. He knew he was just grasping at straws. At the same time, though, he had come all this distance to speak with that girl, and he was not going to give up on the idea now. So without more contemplation, he began pounding on the main door in hopes someone inside might hear him.

Paul had been banging on the door for several minutes, when he finally got an answer. Somebody appeared, and it was the girl Paul had come to see. Only this time, she wasn't wearing her flashy poncho. Instead, she was clad in only a plain sweater and a pair of blue jeans. She came out carrying a couple of boxes in her arms. When she heard the commotion Paul was making, she set her packages on a table and went over to the door. When she saw who it was, she unlocked the door and opened it.

"Hi," she said softly. "What brings you here?"

Paul was a bit shocked by this greeting, since this girl had invited him here in the first place. "What's going on?" he asked. "Where are all the people?"

The girl hesitated a moment and then sighed. "Oh, nobody comes here anymore."

"What?" Paul exclaimed. "Isn't the place still open?"

"No, it isn't." She forced a hint of a laugh.

"What happened?" Paul inquired, still baffled.

The girl, glassy-eyed as ever, seemed more serene and coherent than she had been either of the times when Paul had seen her before. As a matter of fact, to Paul, she seemed downright despondent. She let out another depressed sigh and looked at Paul with a serious expression. "Do you want to sit down and talk for a while?" she asked.

Paul nodded, and the girl opened the door all the way to let him in. After she closed the door, she led Paul to a table. They took chairs off a table, and both sat down.

"The Flock Together has been closed for good," she explained. "I'm just here to get some things packed up and moved out."

Paul couldn't believe his ears. "The Flock Together has been closed down?" he repeated. "How on earth did that happen?"

Looking down, the girl reluctantly began her story. "A couple of weeks ago, not long after the last time I saw you here, the place was busted," she said. "It was a Friday night, and the normal activities were going on, when all of a sudden five cops broke in, went through every square foot of the joint, and searched everybody in this goddamn place. Anybody who was caught with dope on them or who was already turned on was taken in and booked immediately. Everybody else was thrown out on the double. A couple of days later, the head of the police department in Greensboro ordered the whole place to be shut down permanently."

Paul remembered the condition this girl had been in the last time he saw her. It crossed his mind that she should have been one of the first to be hauled away. "But what happened to you?" he questioned. "Weren't you booked or taken in or anything?"

"No," the girl answered. "Luckily, I wasn't working that night. Even so, the whole thing is a big letdown for me. Among other things, I don't have a job anymore since this place has been shut down."

"What are you going to do now?"

"I don't know. I honestly don't know. That's the whole problem." Then she changed the subject. "So you didn't answer my question, kid. What did you come here for today?"

Paul, feeling rather embarrassed about his purpose for coming, did not know where to begin. "For one thing," he started out. "I came to see you."

The girl looked at Paul suspiciously. "Yeah," she laughed. "But there's more to your visit than that. I can tell. There's something else you want from me."

Oh, boy, Paul thought. This girl was smarter than he had thought all along. She knew from the start that there was some special motive for his coming to see her, even before he gave her the slightest notion about it. Paul figured he might as well acknowledge what his friend seemed to know anyway.

"OK," he confessed. "I'll level with you. There is something I need that I think you may be able to get for me."

"Oh, really?" the girl responded. "What is it you need that you think I might have?"

"I need a gun," Paul replied bluntly. "Preferably a pistol, but any kind of gun will do. Do you know somebody who might have one?"

The girl seemed neither shocked nor surprised by Paul's request. She had no intention of asking him what he needed the weapon for. Instead, she simply chose to answer Paul's question.

"Yes," she said calmly. "As a matter of fact, I do. I have friends who are politically involved. They have connections to all kinds of weapons, and pistols are one of the easiest things for them to get."

When he heard that, Paul almost laughed out loud. Friends who are politically involved, he thought. Paul was sure that these "friends" were either communists or terrorists—or both. But that was her business. As long as he got what he wanted, he didn't care where it came from.

"That's great," Paul said. "How long do you think it will take before you can make arrangements with these friends of yours?"

"Oh, I don't know," she said casually. "A week, maybe longer. But in the meantime, I'm going to need a deposit from you."

"A deposit from me?" he asked. "How much of a deposit?"

"Oh, the gun will cost about $100," the girl figured. "But $50 will do for the time being. This is to make sure you come back once I've bought the thing."

How terribly kind of her, Paul mused. Now his little girlfriend wanted a deposit for an illegal weapon. Less than a month ago, she was telling Paul that she didn't care about anybody's money. What a damn hypocrite, he concluded. Nevertheless, Paul realized that if he wanted to get that gun from her, he would have to abide by his faithful comrade's wishes. So he half-heartedly reached into his back pocket and pulled out his wallet. He opened it and pulled out two twenties and a ten-dollar bill. Then he tossed the money on the table.

When she saw what Paul had just offered her, the girl slid the bills off the table. "Very good," she said. "I'll see what I can do within the next couple of days. How about if you stop by this place next week at this time?"

"OK," Paul agreed. "But are you sure you'll be here next week?"

"I'll make it," she promised him. "For such a special occasion, I'll make it." Then she gave Paul a sly grin.

"OK. "I'll come back exactly a week from today."

"Very good. I'll be waiting for you here next week. But remember one thing. When I get that gun, I'll be expecting another fifty bucks from you."

"All right," Paul agreed. "By that time I will have found some way to get the rest of the money."

After his friend rather formally led him to the door and opened it, she stood out of the way for Paul to leave. As he walked out the door, the girl made no effort to be kind or friendly with him. Instead, she simply reminded him again of their next rendezvous.

"Remember," she told him. "Next week at the exact same time, I'll be here waiting for you."

"All right," Paul said again. Then he walked out the door.

As he walked to his car, Paul thought about it. He couldn't help but notice how the girl had changed since the last time he saw her. Within less than a month, she had gone from amiable and outgoing to cool and calculating. Was it the fact that Paul now depended on her—or was it that her unfortunate circumstances had suddenly altered her disposition? It was probably for both reasons, Paul assumed.

At any rate, Paul didn't care how the girl related to him—now or before. As long as he got what he wanted from her, she could relate any way she wanted to him. In a way, Paul felt relieved to know that this girl did have access to what he needed and that she would be able to get it for him in time. Therefore, Paul was sure that the job would be finished before it was too late.

Paul was almost smiling as he walked up to his car, got inside, and drove away.

As planned, Paul went back to the place one week later. When he arrived, he found the main door locked as before. Since the girl was expecting him, however, Paul knocked until he got an answer, and this time it wasn't long before he did. The girl came out into the room only a few seconds after hearing him knocking on the door. This time she knew who it was. She unlocked the door to let Paul in.

"Hi," she said.

Since the girl knew exactly why Paul had come to see her, she wasted no time in getting down to business. "Why don't you have a seat?" she suggested as she pointed to one of the tables. "I'll be back in a minute." Then she left the room.

Paul was a bit stunned by the girl's quick actions. But as always, he wasn't displeased. As long as he got what he came there for, he was not about to complain. When she returned, the girl was carrying a paper bag that had something inside. It was cinch for Paul to guess what it was. She went over to Paul and set the bag on the table. Judging by the sound the contents of the bag made as it was placed on the table, Paul could safely conclude that it was exactly what he had requested. The girl then pulled out a chair and sat down across from Paul.

"Take a look," she told him, as she leaned back in her seat. "See if that's what you wanted."

Paul picked the heavy bag off the table and opened it. He reached in and pulled out what looked to him to be a compact pistol. The girl watched Paul as he looked the weapon over, feeling it up and down with his fingers as if it were some magnificent object. When she saw this, the girl could not help but be a bit curious as to why Paul wanted this pistol in the first place. Still, she refrained from any unnecessary probing.

"What do you think?" she asked. "Is it to your satisfaction?"

"It sure is," Paul smiled, as he continued looking the pistol over.

The girl felt it was time to remind Paul of the balance he owed her. "You remember our deal, don't you?" she said. "Fifty more dollars once I got the thing."

Paul broke out of what seemed almost a daze. "Oh, yeah," he recalled. "Don't worry. I brought it with me."

Paul reached into his back pocket and once again pulled out his wallet. This time he pulled out a single fifty-dollar bill. After he tossed it onto the table, he put his wallet back. "So we're even," he affirmed, looking up at the girl.

"Yes, of course," the girl told him, picking the money off the table. "I got you what you wanted, and you've paid me. A deal's a deal."

Once the transaction was done, Paul got up and prepared to leave. He picked up the paper bag, placed the gun inside it, wrapped the bag tightly around the pistol, and tucked it under his arm. As he headed for the door, the girl did the same. As she opened the door to let Paul out, she bade him one last good-bye.

"Good luck," she said, warming up a bit.

"Thanks," he said. "And thanks a whole lot for helping me."

"Oh, any time," the girl volunteered, trying to force a slight smile.

"Sure, any time," Paul agreed, making an effort to humor the girl.

Finally, after Paul walked out the door, the girl closed and locked it behind him. Paul looked back one last time and waved to the girl through the window. After she waved back, he turned and left the building, knowing this time that he would never, ever return.

A few days after he had bought the pistol, Paul tied up all the loose ends of his carefully constructed plan. He purchased several bullets for the gun and made arrangements to bid his last farewell to his mother. He also laid plans to make sure that his Aunt Addie was out of the house when he carried out the last part of his plan.

Today, ironically enough, was Paul's twenty-sixth birthday. It would also be his death day. Everything seemed so nice, neat, and well-arranged—so much the opposite from the way things had been before. It seemed obvious that would be the perfect suicide. Nothing would go wrong. Nothing.

Paul decided to call his mother at an early hour when she was sure to be at home. As far as Louise was concerned, Paul might call her up to say "hell," and that would be the extent of it. So around 8 a.m., Paul crept down the stairs, hoping not to attract the attention of Addie, who was already sitting in the library reading. Paul went to the phone sitting on a small table in the main hallway and picked up the receiver. With his other hand, he reluctantly dialed his mother's number. After four or five rings, Paul got an answer.

"Hello?" Louise said in a hoarse voice.

"Hello," her son replied. "This is Paul."

"Oh, hi, Paul," Louise greeted him. "What's up?"

"Nothing's up," Paul said. "I called to tell you that things are fine over here."

"Oh, that's good," Louise commented. "By the way, did you go see the social worker last week?"

"Yes, I—I did," Paul stuttered. Paul was not expecting his mother to bring this up. So now he could not help but sound a bit fidgity.

"What did he say?" Louise asked anxiously.

"Oh, nothing much," Paul said evasively. "We had the usual session, that's all."

"But your counselor must have said something about your progress," Louise insisted. "Didn't he make any kind of analysis or anything?"

"Yes," Paul confessed. "As a matter of fact, he did. He said that I might have to go back into the hospital if I don't improve quickly."

"Oh," Louise moaned. But before she had a chance to say another word, Paul interrupted his mother's sorrowful mood.

"But don't worry about it, Mom," he assured her. "Because I'm not going back there." His voice was surprisingly firm and decisive.

"You're not?" Louise questioned in a confused tone.

"No," Paul confirmed. "I'm not ever going back there, no matter what happens."

For Paul's sake, Louise chose not to push the matter any further. She did not understand exactly what her son was trying to tell her, but she did realize that asking for explanations would probably do more harm than good. So for the time being, Louise just assumed that Paul was rationalizing his way out of a painful situation and that they should just leave it at that.

"All right," she relented. "We'll see what happens later on."

"Yes," Paul said. "We'll definitely see what happens."

Recalling that this was a long distance telephone call that would show up on Addie's phone bill at the end of the month, Louise subtly elected to call the conversation to an end. "Hey, listen, Paul," she whispered. "I think we'd better sign off now. These long distance calls cost, you know."

"Yeah," Paul agreed. "You're right about that."

"But thank you for calling, Paul," Louise said, trying to sound as appreciative as possible.

"Yeah, any time," Paul obliged, using the same pretense of goodwill that his mother had just employed. "Goodbye, Mom."

"Goodbye, son," Louise replied.

Addie had not been listening to the conversation out in the hallway. She was too busy trying to make out the small print of the paperback book she was reading through her magnifying glass. She did, however, notice that Louise hadn't said anything about Paul's birthday. Addie excused her. It must have slipped her mind. It was a shame, nevertheless, Addie thought, for Paul's mother to forget his birthday. It crossed her mind that she should go out herself and buy Paul a present. Addie set her book and magnifying glass on the coffee table and walked into the hallway. There she found Paul still standing by the phone.

"Paul," she said as she stood near the doorway to the library. "I'm going out for a while. I'll be back in about a half hour."

Paul slowly turned toward Addie as she groped her way to the hallway closet. "Good," he responded. "Take your time."

"OK," Addie replied.

The old lady reached up to get her black handbag on the top shelf of the hallway closet. When she got it down, she slipped her hand inside to make sure she had enough money. Then she picked up her laser cane, which was leaning against the wall, and felt her way to the front door. She slowly opened it and walked out of the house.

Paul stared slyly at the woman as she closed the door behind her. Oh, goodness, he thought. A half hour of solitude. A half hour of seclusion. A half hour of utter privacy. What could be more perfect? Paul knew that he would do it. Whether he was ready or not, he would do it.

Paul hesitated as he stood there at the bottom of the staircase. Finally he reached his hand around the circular railing and started walking upstairs. For some strange reason, climbing those stairs never seemed so long and tiring as it did today. He puffed and panted as he went from one step to another of the relatively short staircase. Once he reached the top, Paul stopped cold for a moment. He stood there, staring at the open doorway to his bedroom. The sunlight glowed mysteriously into the shadowed upstairs. As he observed this strange lighting, Paul could barely find the courage to go inside his own bedroom. What he saw there haunted him terribly. But after pondering for only a few seconds, Paul forced himself to walk over to the door of his bedroom, go inside, and close it.

He immediately went over to his desk and opened up the top drawer. Inside lay the compact pistol, brand-new and ready to use. It was, in fact, already loaded. For a minute or two, Paul stared at the open drawer, looking intently at what was inside it. His breathing became incredibly long and heavy as he took the weapon in his hand and walked over to the edge of his unmade bed.

When Paul felt he was composed enough to follow through with his ingenious plan, he took the pistol and wrapped his right hand around the handle. He placed his forefinger inside the loop near the trigger. He sat up straight and tall as he closed his eyes and took one last deep breath. He held the gun up to his temple and pulled the trigger.

Silence. There was complete silence inside the house when Addie came in the door less than a half hour later. She was holding a small, carefully wrapped package under her arm. The minute Addie got inside, she found one of her black cats in the hallway, staring at her nervously from behind the staircase. He seemed to have been frightened badly by something—so frightened, in fact, that he disappeared into the library as soon as Addie came into the hallway.

Addie closed the door behind her and placed the gift-wrapped package on the small table next to the stairs. Assuming that Paul was in his bedroom, Addie decided to call him so that he would come out.

"Paul," she called out. "Come down here for a second. I have something here for you."

Addie waited a few seconds. Getting no response, she called again. "Paul... Paul!" she repeated. "Are you up there?" Still no answer.

Finally, the old lady proceeded to climb the stairs to see if Paul was in his bedroom or not. She took the present from the hallway table and tucked it conveniently under her arm again. She then started cautiously walking up the stairs. As she climbed the staircase, she hesitated every inch of the way, feeling and groping with her laser cane before she took each step. When she got upstairs, Addie noticed that Paul's bedroom door was shut. This struck her as rather odd. Paul rarely kept his bedroom door closed during the day. Even so, Addie thought it wise to call him one more time before she went into his room.

"Paul," she yelled from the top of the stairs. "Are you there?" Still no response.

At last the woman took it on herself to approach the closed door and tap on it a few times. When she got no answer, Addie almost apprehensively decided to enter Paul's room. She took her free hand and reached for the doorknob, grasping it and turning it carefully until the door cracked open. Pushing lightly, she made the door swing open.

As she looked toward the bed, all that the old lady could see was a listless body sprawled out on top of it, still holding a pistol in one hand. The face was completely white, the mouth open, and the eyes staring blankly at the ceiling.

Chapter 16

Anna was still in Tunis, quite unaware of anything happening outside of her own private life. She'd been dismissed from her precious teaching job, and she had absolutely no idea of where to go from here. Once she had overcome the shock, though, Anna was glad to have lost her job. She felt relieved about not having to go back to such an unpleasant situation. Besides, Anna knew deep inside that things would not have changed if she had gone back.

Anna still could not forget that she had been tormented, humiliated, and defeated by all those people around her throughout this whole ordeal. Now she could seek her revenge. Now she would display her personality for what it really was. Now Anna could ridicule and embarrass those people who had done the same to her.

Anna's first order of business was to make clear to everybody at the Institute that she did not give a damn about being fired. So only a few days after she had received the appalling letter from the superintendent, Anna dared to go back, smiling ear-to-ear.

Before she could enter the building, Anna encountered the dreadful female coordinator. As usual, she did not have a kind word to say to Anna. She merely turned up her nose and greeted Anna with a cool "bon jour." From that moment, not only was Anna sure that this woman knew about her termination, she also had reason to believe that she was one of the people responsible for that crucial decision. Even so, Anna felt profoundly content. When she passed the woman on the street, Anna threw her way nothing less than a sadistic grin. She knew that the coordinator understood immediately that Anna was much happier with her new circumstances than she had been in her old situation.

At the Institute Anna went directly to Ben Hassen's office showing neither self consciousness or reservation. But once he saw who had come to see him, Ben Hassen did not look up again as he was sitting at his desk.

"Hello," Anna greeted him cheerfully.

"Hello," he said, still looking down at his desk. "What can I do for you today?"

"I was wondering if it would be possible to receive my mail here over the summer," Anna told him.

Ben Hassen could not help but show signs of curiosity. "Why would you want to do that?" he asked, peering at Anna out of the corner of his eye.

Anna decided to take advantage of this golden opportunity to show the administrator exactly where she was coming from. "Well," she smiled sweetly. "If I'm not going to be working here next year, I've got to start looking for something else. To do that, I'll need to make arrangements by mail. That's why I want to be able to get my mail here." That, she thought, was clear enough.

Ben Hassen's eyes stared straight ahead, avoiding any possible visual contact with Anna. "Yes, I can understand that," he replied. "Certainly you can pick up your mail here over the summer, as you would any other time of the year. The Institute is open all year, you know."

"Good," Anna said. "I wanted to make sure, that's all." Anna opened the office door. "Thank you," she said to Ben Hassen before she left his office. Ben Hassen, however, said nothing as he watched her walk out.

From there, Anna went down to the first floor, where she was immediately greeted by a group of her students. As usual, they crowded around her like a flock of sheep. Judging from their behavior,

Anna got the distinct impression that they hadn't heard what had happened to her. How ironic, she thought, since they were the ones she wanted to get even with most of all. They thought that they were so smart all year, she mused. Well, let them see what they've done now. Let them see what kind of teacher and companion they have lost. But let's not do it right away, Anna decided. Instead, she thought she would give them a little line and then let them suffer the shock the following year. In a nutshell, Anna knew that soon the joke would be on them.

Before she even had the chance to think of what to say to them, one of her students brought up the subject she had just been reflecting on.

"You are coming back next year, aren't you?" he asked with anticipation.

Anna did not answer that question right away. Instead, she thought about it for a few seconds and then replied. "Oh, yes," she responded decisively. "Of course I'll be coming back next year. I'll see you then." Then she walked away from all of them.

As she was leaving the Institute that day, Anna thought about it. Why did she act so blatantly with the coordinator? How was it that she was so frank and straightforward with Ben Hassen? And why did she turn around and lie to her students? She was certainly not out to mislead anybody about anything. On the contrary, she wanted everybody to know the truth. Actually, what Anna had just done was to engage in a subtle form of mockery. It was her way of evening the score for everything that had been done to her throughout the year. So it seemed that in a sense, this scheme had worked for Anna.

The next day Anna went back to the Institute to pick up her last paycheck. As soon as she entered the office that handled payroll, she met two young clerks she thought she didn't know. Surprisingly to her, though, they were quite friendly to her. This was possibly the first time during the whole year that anyone other than her students had made any attempt to be gracious or personable with her.

After he had given her the paycheck, one of the clerks asked Anna the expected question. "Are you coming back next year?" he inquired.

Anna gave the man a meek smile and shook her head. "No," she answered. "I'm not coming back."

The other clerk, looking rather confused, asked her the next-most-obvious question. "But I thought that the contracts for all foreign teachers were for two years," he said. "Haven't you been here for only one?"

"Yes, as a matter of fact, I have. But I have been told that my services here are no longer needed for next year."

"Who told you that?" the first clerk asked.

Anna smiled meekly and shook her head. "I'm not really sure," she explained. "All I know is that I got a letter from the superintendent here in Tunis telling me that I had been fired. Who gave him the idea to do that, I never bothered to find out, but I assume it was the director."

When they heard this, the two men could not help but show a half-disgusted expression. Anna figured that they probably got along with the director about as well as she did. Furthermore, Anna got the distinct impression that these guys were fairly sympathetic with the circumstances under which Anna found herself.

"We're very sorry to hear that," one of them told her.

Anna grinned one last time. "Don't be," she advised them. "I was having so many problems here that I suppose it's for the best."

The two men returned Anna's pleasant expression, almost as if they understood exactly what she meant. They both shook Anna's hand and bade her a fond farewell.

As Anna walked out of the Institute that day, she felt even more satisfied than she had the day before. This was the first time since she had been inside the building that Anna felt she'd been able to relate to anybody on an intimate basis. It was also the first time she'd felt on fairly good terms with the people around her. Anna knew that she had finally broken the barrier between herself and what the Institute had represented to her from the moment she had set foot inside the building at the beginning of the school year.

Soon enough, through subtle hints and rumors, everybody in the Institute's administration heard about what had happened to Anna. Everybody had gotten the word, that is, except for the man responsible for it. Finally, though, the director's attention would inevitably be drawn to his previous decision.

The director knew that Anna was too shrewd to stomp into his office and fight him head on. He also knew that Anna was smart enough to recognize that no matter what she did, the director would never change his mind and reverse his decision. But what the director did not realize was that Anna was still out to seek revenge. One of her ulterior motives for subtly letting everyone know what had transpired with her job was to embarrass the director. Within a matter of days after she had discovered that she had been fired, Anna had related it to all the main personnel in the establishment. In this way, she assumed that the word would get back to the man who would tell the director as quickly as possible—Ben Hassen.

Barely a week after Anna's brief discussions with practically everybody at the Institute, Ben Hassen finally felt so perturbed that he thought he had better take the matter up with the director. Ben Hassen rushed into his office without so much as making an appointment to see him. Noticing

Ben Hassen's nervous and fidgity behavior, the director stood up the moment he entered his office.

"Hello, what brings you here at this time?" he said.

Ben Hassen sat down in front of him. "I was kind of wondering," he started out, "has that Miss Daleddo been in to see you lately?"

The director sat down and thought a bit. "No," he answered. "As a matter of fact, she hasn't. Why?"

"Because she's going around telling everybody what happened." There was almost an element of panic in Ben Hassen's voice. "What's more, she says that you're the one responsible, but that she doesn't care, and that she didn't like it here, and so on."

"So what about it?" the director retorted coldly.

"So now everybody knows it. That's what about it!" The way Ben Hassen described the whole incident, it seemed as if it could have been something to go in the newspapers.

The director was listening to everything Ben Hassen was telling him, but he showed no outward reaction. "My friend," he addressed his colleague. "Don't worry about it. The girl has been terminated. She is no longer working here. That's all there is to it."

Ben Hassen calmed down a bit, as he was convinced that the director was not affected by this news. "All right," he agreed. "I just wanted you to know what was going on."

The director sighed as he leaned back in his chair. "As I have said, Ben Hassen, you don't have to worry about a thing," he assured him. "Miss Daleddo is through, and that is that."

Ben Hassen sat up straight, trying to display an air of confidence and self assurance. "I guess you're right," he said. "The decision has been made, and that's the end of it. She can't do anything about it."

"No, I'm sure she can't," the director agreed. "If you'll excuse me, Ben Hassen, I have some pressing work I need to finish by this afternoon."

Ben Hassen almost jumped with embarrassment. "Oh, of course," he said. He walked to the door, turned to the director and said, "I just wanted you to know. That's all." Then he walked out of the office.

As soon as Ben Hasen had left, the director started swiveling nervously in his executive leather chair. The more he thought about it, the more agitated he became. Why, that little sneak, he thought to himself. She is out to make a fool of me. Now he could admit it. Now that he was alone, he could let all of his emotions surface. The director turned and twitched some more in his huge armchair.

He realized now that Anna was even smarter than he had thought. She had done it, the director concluded. She had put him in such a light that he looked bad to everybody in the establishment. He shifted and swiveled in his chair and thought about it some more. Really, he wondered. What makes this lady's mind work?

That evening, Anna was anticipating a visit from Noureddine, whom she had not seen in quite some time. The basic reason for this was that they were both preoccupied with their own problems—Anna with the termination of her job, and Noureddine with his final exams, some of which he had to retake. Noureddine spent almost every day studying, either in the library or in his tiny room. Anna, of course, understood his temporary absence from her life. Nonetheless, at a time such as this, she really did feel she could use some company. So after waiting patiently for what had seemed a very long time, Anna was thrilled that tonight Noureddine was coming over to see her.

That evening they sat alone in Anna's small, but attractively decorated kitchen. They were eating dinner at a round table that could only accommodate two people sitting and facing each other. All of a sudden, Noureddine abruptly dropped his fork onto the empty plate in front of him. He had finished his dinner.

"Annie," he said in a serious tone of voice. "I've got to go."

Anna's face fell. "It seems like you just got here," she remarked, sounding almost hurt.

"I know, but I've got to get to the library before it closes. There's some last-minute research I have to do for one of my exams this week." Noureddine acted as if he felt terribly guilty.

Anna really was disheartened. Even though she tried to hide her feelings from Noureddine, they showed through anyway. "Go ahead, if you must," she consented, as she revealed her disappointment with a heavy sigh.

"I'm sorry, Annie," Noureddine apologized again. "But you know that this is a bad time for me. I'm taking all my tests now, and my degree depends on how well I do on them."

"Yeah, I know," Anna excused him. "I guess it's a bad time for both of us." Noureddine's explanations seemed trivial to her, and Anna's dismissals as well appeared to be meaningless.

Before Anna could try to talk him into staying at least a little longer, Noureddine got up from his seat and walked to the other side of the table. He put his hands on Anna's shoulders and then bent over, giving her a tender kiss. "I'll see you," he said softly, trying to overcompensate for his actions.

Anna, still frowning, did not budge from her seat. "Yeah, maybe," she retorted, making no effort to hide her feelings of resentment.

Noureddine hesitated a moment, then left the kitchen and went into the hallway. Without another word, he grabbed some books he had brought with him, opened the door, and walked out. When Anna heard the door slam shut behind him, she forced herself to get up and started cleaning off the table.

Once Anna had gathered all the dishes and taken them to the sink, she began washing them. Noureddine wasn't going to spend the night, and the other girl in her apartment had gone to visit her parents for a couple of days. Anna would be completely alone tonight. The more she thought about it, the more the idea frightened her. This was rather strange, since normally she was not afraid either of the night or of being alone. Tonight, however, was different.

Anna closed the kitchen, put all the food and dishes away, and turned off the lights. She went into her room, where she stretched out on her bed and picked up a paperback book resting on her night table. She opened it to the page where the bookmark was keeping her place. Then she rustled through the pages she had yet to read. She was only about halfway through the book. Ugh, she thought. Another night with nothing better to do than read some corny novel about love and romance.

But what was the difference now? It was finally the end of the year. It was all over for her. Besides, Anna had already spent a thousand nights like this. A thousand nights, she thought. What difference does one more make? None, she concluded. Absolutely none. Just the same, Anna had the strangest feeling that something odd was going to happen before the night was over. Tonight would be different for her—Anna was sure of it.

Anna had been reading quite a while before she finally stopped to get ready for bed. She went over to her chest and opened it. Still facing the open chest, she began to undress. She took off every piece of clothing she was wearing, folded it carefully, and placed it inside her chest. Then she reached up to the top shelf and pulled out her white nightgown, which she unfolded and put on.

Now Anna was ready for bed. She was not tired, but she felt that she had nothing better to do than at least try to get some sleep. She sighed hesitantly as she went over to her bed and pulled the covers down about halfway. She sat at the edge of the mattress and reached for the light on her night table. She turned it off and stretched out, pulling the covers up over her.

In total darkness, Anna lay there alone. She was not sleepy—she was not even tired. Anna knew she would not be able to fall asleep right away. She was not even sure she would be able to fall asleep at all. The more she lay there awake, the more the feeling of solitude crept over her, making her want so much to be somewhere else with somebody else. But instead, she just lay there by herself, with no one near.

The only thing Anna could hear was the ticking of the noisy alarm clock on her night table. It ticked boldly and insolently by her side. Tick-tock, tick-tock, tick-tock, counting the time that had already passed—seconds, minutes, hours. Yes. Hours had now passed. One o'clock, two o'clock, three o'clock in the morning. Yet Anna lay there with her eyes open, her breath heavy, her mind and body exhausted with insomnia, but still unable to sleep. So she just lay there, completely still, completely sedate, completely alone.

Tick-tock, tick-tock, tick-tock. It was now three-thirty in the morning, and Anna was still wide awake. She was expecting no interruption during this prolonged sleeplessness. All of a sudden, a strange and frightful sound caught her attention. It was so loud, so abrupt, so unsubtle, that Anna jumped when she heard it. It was the telephone ringing in the hallway.

Anna was so shocked to be hearing the telephone at this time in the morning that she did not turn on the light before she stumbled out of bed and ran to the door. She opened it and hurried to the phone beside it. Before she had time to think about who could be calling her at this hour of the morning, she had grabbed the receiver and held it up to her ear.

"Hello?...Oh, hello, Mother...What's the matter?... What is it?... But you must tell me." Then Anna slowly lowered the telephone receiver from her ear, displaying the most terrified expression. "Oh, God!" she gasped.

Tick-tock, tick-tock, tick-tock. Time lagged as Anna and her mother talked, exchanging condolences, comforting each other, saying things that didn't really make much sense at all. Time dragged slowly on as it normally would, without interruption, without end.

"Don't worry about it, Mother. Everything is going to be all right...Yeah, I know...Yes, and give my love to everybody, will you?...All right...Good-bye, Mother."

Anna waited a few seconds, staring at the phone. But when she heard the telephone click, she slowly hung it up. For a few seconds, Anna was unable to move, incapable of making a choice about what to do next. She just stood there next to the phone, unable to think, reason, or decide. Then Anna recalled that she was still completely alone—with no one around her.

If there had been one other person there with her, Anna would not have done what she was about to do right then. But now she would react dramatically, drastically, and violently. Now Anna would do what she felt she had to do.

Before she had time to think about it, Anna went back to her bedroom, turned on the light, and hurried over to her chest, where she opened the door. Rushed and panic-stricken, she pulled out all the clothes she had so neatly folded and arranged earlier and threw them out on the floor. She pulled her nightgown up over her head and flung it down on the floor as well. Quickly, and with no rhyme or reason, she got dressed, not paying much attention to the fit or order of her clothes.

She grabbed her house keys, which were on one of the shelves in her chest, and ran into the hallway. Not bothering even to turn off her bedroom light, she opened the main door in the hallway and went out, slamming the door behind her. Without turning on the lights on the stairway of the apartment building, Anna groped her way down two flights of steps, appearing to know her way even in the dark. When she got to the bottom of the stairs, she felt for the deadlock to open the outside door. She unlatched the door, opened it quickly, and went outside.

It was clear and warm outside, as it was July—and it was nearly four in the morning.

Chapter 17

So that's how it happened?" Noureddine said, summing up what Anna had just told him there in the café.

"That's how they say it happened, from what little they know about it," Anna replied, now acting considerably more coherent than she had been a while ago.

Noureddine looked at Anna intently. "Is this really the end for you—or is it perhaps the beginning?" he challenged her, trying as much as possible to direct her attention away from what they had been talking about before.

Anna looked up at her friend with surprise. "What is that supposed to mean?" she asked in a low, suspicious voice.

Noureddine leaned forward in his seat and looked into Anna's eyes. "Annie," he said softly. "Stay with me. I want you to marry me. I mean it this time. Stay here in Tunisia with me. There's nothing for you to go home to anyway."

When she heard what Noureddine had told her, Anna laughed to herself. "But there's nothing for me here either," she argued. "I don't even have a job any more."

"Oh, don't worry about that," he assured her. "This year I should have my degree. If all goes well next year, I'll have my master's. Then I'll get a job. I'm sure that by that time you'll be able to find another job. We'll make some money between the two of us. We'll make a life together. Once we're a little settled, we can go to the U.S."

Anna smiled. "Are you sure about what you want to do this time?" she said, sounding a bit skeptical about what he was telling her.

"Yes, I'm positive," he insisted. "I'm deadly serious about everything I'm saying to you."

A full, satisfied smile spread over Anna's face. She could not help but show pleasure in hearing what she had wanted to hear for such a long time. In spite of the fact that Anna knew that what she was being promised today could easily turn into futile lies tomorrow, she was happy. She was content to realize there was at least a ray of hope for her future, and for the time being Anna would consider it just that—hope.

"Tell you what, Noureddine," she said. "Let me sleep on it. It's too early to give you an answer right away, you know. I'll need at least twenty-four hours to think it over." Then Anna giggled lightly.

"OK," he smiled. "But remember one thing. I really mean everything I'm telling you right now. I want you to stay with me. I want you to be my wife. I'm sure of it."

Anna laughed out loud. "You know something, dear?"

"What's that?"

"You always make my day so much brighter—even today." Then she smiled again.

After leaving the café, the two of them went back to Noureddine's room. When Anna sat on Noureddine's bed, propped up with some pillows and staring across the room, while Noureddine was downstairs at a neighbor's place making some coffee. When he came back to the room, Noureddine had two glasses in his hand. He handed one of them to Anna. Then he sat in front of her.

"Annie," he said. "What are you thinking about?'

This seemed like a banal question to Anna. "It may surprise you," she sighed. "But I'm thinking about my parents."

"Really? What are your thoughts about them?"

"I'm thinking that it would be rather selfish to leave them alone at a time like this." Then she looked at Noureddine straight in the eye. "Wouldn't you say so?"

"Annie," Noureddine said again. "You've got to worry about you first. Your parents can take care of themselves."

"Worrying about my parents is the same as worrying about me," she argued. "They are my parents. I'm sure they need me now. Yes, I believe I must go back to them. Whether we get married later on or not, I must go back to my parents now."

Noureddine was obviously uncomfortable with this idea, as he could never be sure that Anna would come back once she left him. "But could you tell me one thing?" he questioned her.

"Of course," Anna replied.

"Do you still love me?"

"Of course, I do," Anna declared. "You must know that."

"Then why do you want to leave me instead of staying here and marrying me?"

Anna felt as if she had been put on the spot. "Noureddine," she said. "The answer to that question should be obvious to you. We're different in so many ways, my dear. We vary in everything from skin color to political ideas."

Noureddine was shocked and insulted by that comment. "What is that supposed to mean?" he said in an angry voice. "How could the two of us be that different?"

Anna looked Noureddine straight in the eye again. "Let's face it, sweetheart," she said. "We are different. We would have to be. We come from two different worlds."

"So what?" Noureddine said. "That doesn't mean we can't overcome those differences."

"I suppose not, but you can still understand why I'm apprehensive about it." Then Anna recalled that they had gotten completely off the subject they had previously been talking about. "By the way," she commented. "I don't know how we got so sidetracked. Remember that we were talking about my parents."

"Don't worry about it, Annie," Noureddine assured her. "I'm sure everything is going to work out fine."

Then Anna forced a subtle smile. "After all I've been through, somehow I believe you."

Without saying anything more, they both drank their coffee.

After resting a bit in Noureddine's room, he and Anna went for a walk up to the Souks, which were not at all that far from where he lived. It crossed Anna's mind that her unexpected state of grief was detaining Noureddine from his pressing studies, but he said that he didn't mind staying with her at all. Besides, he had been studying hard all the week before and was ready for a break anyway.

The two of them were walking up the cobblestone alleys and browsing around in the various shops, when suddenly Anna recognized the store where she had bought a painting when she first found her apartment. Spotting the two young salesmen who had sold her the painting, Anna decided that she wanted to take a peek inside one more time. She stopped and turned to Noureddine.

"I want to go in here for a moment," she told him. They both went inside the shop.

When they saw Anna enter the store, both the young salesmen seemed to recognize her right away. They also looked eager to try and sell her something else. Anna and Noureddine, began checking out the merchandise in the store, looking mostly at the paintings sold there. After seeing nothing on the wall that appealed to her, Anna started thumbing through a few of the stacks on the floor. When she came to the third pile, Anna finally found a picture that interested her. It was a peaceful scene—a lake reflecting the sunlight, surrounded by woods and greenery. For some reason, Anna liked this painting very much. She liked it so much, in fact, that she decided she had to have it. So she went up to one of the salesmen and began bidding for it.

"How much do you want for this picture?" she asked coldly.

"A hundred dinars," he blurted out, sounding as if he would not budge from that price.

Anna lifted her chin and straightened her body. "I will pay no more than sixty dinars," she announced.

"Sixty dinars?" quoted the other boy. "Are you crazy? This is an original."

Yeah, I bet it is, Anna thought to herself. So was that other masterpiece that they sold her. "Sixty dinars," she repeated. "I will go no higher."

"How about ninety dinars?" suggested the first salesman, his attitude already weakening. Anna just shook her head indignantly. "Eighty?" he compromised, hoping she would settle for such a bargain. But Anna continued to shake her head, not budging from her original price.

Then the salesman gave a defeated sigh. "All right," he said disgustedly. "But I'll tell you one thing. If all the customers were like you, this store would have gone out of business long ago."

Anna didn't pay attention to the salesman's brisk remarks. She just nodded slyly at Noureddine as she reached into her purse and pulled out her money. She then handed over sixty dinars to the salesman. The young man, in turn, practically snapped it out of her hand.

"Thank you so much," he said sarcastically.

Anna did not reciprocate to that act of rudeness. Instead, she took the painting as it was and left the shop, with Noureddine following close behind her. Then they started walking back down through the Souks. As they passed other shops and stores Noureddine felt that he had to commend Anna for her recent accomplishment.

"Wow," he confessed. "You really got a bargain that time. I'd say that you made out like a bandit."

Anna almost stopped in her tracks. Noureddine was so hypercritical with Anna and rarely paid her any compliments. That comment astounded her. Still, she kept her reaction to herself.

"Yeah," she agreed. "I guess I did."

But as they walked down to the end of the Souks and back to the Medina, Anna laughed to herself. She had to give herself a pat on the back. She had profited from the sale more than the salesmen themselves. Now Anna knew she was no longer apt to be cheated or swindled as she had been before. She was also sure that she would never let herself be taken advantage of in the way that she had been all during the past year. Anna was no longer the weak and naive person she had been. Somehow, Anna knew that things would be different from now on. This whole tragic experience had changed her for the better. Anna was sure of it.

As they were walking back through the Medina, Anna felt even more amused. If only Noureddine knew the truth, she thought. If only he realized that, less than a year ago in that very shop, it was Anna who had gotten burned!

Anna and Noureddine spent the whole day together, walking around the Souks, the Medina, and the rest of the city. Anna appreciated Noureddine's company at a time like this, especially since she knew that he had a lot of things to do that day. He even promised her that he would stay with her that night and on nights to come, if need be. Anna was not about to turn down his companionship, if it were offered to her so willingly. So that evening, they went back to Anna's apartment together.

When they first got to her place, they both had a shot of whiskey. The two of them were in Anna's bedroom, with Anna sitting on a chair and Noureddine stretched out on the bed. They were sipping on their glasses of whiskey, when Noureddine suddenly hit Anna with another question.

"Annie," he said. "What the hell are you thinking about?"

"Oh, nothing much," she sighed. "I was only thinking about how ironic and unpredictable life can be."

"What's that supposed to mean?"

"Oh," Anna sighed again. "I was thinking about this past year and what it all means to me. I was often warned by my father that I was one who would end up six feet underground. He told me that I was going to get raped and murdered." Her tone was obviously sarcastic.

"Fortunately, neither one of those things happened to you."

"I know," Anna granted. "But in a way I wish it had been me. That way I wouldn't be faced with all these decisions."

"Don't ever say that, Annie. I want you to be around for a long time. And besides, what decisions are you talking about? All you have to do is stay here with me. Everything will work out for you. You'll see."

"You seem so sure of that. But what about the differences in lifestyle? What about the adjustments I'm going to have to make?"

"Annie," Noureddine laughed. "You've already made the adjustments. You've been living here for almost a year, you know."

"Yes, but I haven't been your wife. Somehow, I've got the feeling that will be a completely different story."

"Don't worry about it, Annie," Noureddine assured her one more time. "I know that I love you, and you love me, so I'm sure that everything is going to be all right."

Then it was Anna who laughed. "I wish I could be as sure of that as you."

Knowing that they had been through all this before, Noureddine thought it best to change the subject. "How about if we go to bed now?" he said, looking down at his watch. "You're tired, and I'm tired, and it's already eleven o'clock."

Anna didn't feel like sleeping, but she knew that Nouredine was right. They both needed some rest, whether they felt like getting it or not.

"All right," she said. "Let's go to bed."

Within ten minutes, Noureddine had already undressed and gotten into bed. Anna put on her nightgown and stood in front of her chest with a small wooden hairbrush in her hand. As she looked into the large antique mirror on the door of the chest, she thought about it one last time.

What would she do now? What actually were her choices? Would she stay there with the man she loved so much but who had countless chauvinistic ideas and who was from a frightfully traditional background? Or would she go home just to find two grieving and ailing parents with whom she knew she wouldn't want to live, but who needed her so desperately? How could she deal with such disparity?

Anna took the brush and began stroking her hair slowly and evenly. Then she thought about it some more. It was as if she were at some unfamiliar fork in the road, not knowing which direction to take. Anna wanted so much to love and to be loved, but she wanted to do more than this. She wanted to win, to be successful at something, even if it were only one thing. But how in God's name could she win when she had lost just about everything?

She would inevitably succeed, Anna finally concluded. She would find a solution between now and the time she would eventually go home. Suddenly her pensive trance was broken.

"Annie," Noureddine called to her. "Come to bed. You need to get some sleep, you know. I do, too."

Anna looked at him half heartedly. "All right," she said. "I'm coming right away."

Anna stroked her hair a few more times and then opened the door of her chest to put the brush back inside. After closing the chest, she went over to the bed where

Noureddine was already dozing off, and sat down on the edge of it. She reached for the light on the night table and turned it off.

Once Anna had stretched out on the bed, she moved close to Noureddine, who took her in his arms. Anna cuddled up near him and kissed him softly. Feeling soothed and calmed by this closeness, Anna knew she was ready to sleep. So she just lay there, drifting away from all of the fears and anxieties she had experienced for so long. She was completely still, and she knew that Noureddine felt just as pacified by her presence as she was by his.

Soon enough, they both dozed off. They didn't say anything more.